YOUR SEXUAL FREEDOM

Richard Hettlinger

YOUR
SEXUAL
FREEDOM
LETTERS TO STUDENTS

CONTINUUM · NEW YORK

HQ
18
.U5
H46
1982

Grateful acknowledgment is made to Alfred A. Knopf, Inc. for permission
to reprint lines from *The Hite Report on Male Sexuality* by Shere Hite,
copyright © 1978, 1971 by Shere Hite, and to Macmillan Publishing Co.,
Inc. for permission to reprint lines from *The Hite Report: A Nationwide Study
of Female Sexuality* by Shere Hite, copyright © 1976 by Shere Hite.

1982
The Continuum Publishing Company
575 Lexington Avenue
New York, N.Y. 10022

Printed in the United States of America.

Library of Congress Cataloging in Publication Data

Hettlinger, Richard Frederick.
    Your sexual freedom.

    Bibliography: p. 128
    1. Sex customs—United States.   2. College students—
United States—Sexual behavior.   I. Title.
HQ18.U5H46   306.7′088375   81-17379
ISBN 0-8264-0184-8 (pbk.)   AACR2

For G. P. H. and C. S.

CONTENTS

To the Student Reader

My justification for adding to the glut of books on sex is that I believe many students have been promised something they fail to find. You have been invited to celebrate the joys of sex but offered little help in coping with its complexities. You may know a good deal about its immediate pleasures but much less about its deeper satisfactions. Sex can be among the most liberating and enriching of all human experiences, but it can also have frustrating and destructive consequences. The sexual freedom open to students today is something to be enjoyed to the full; but it is a mistake to think of it merely as a matter of acquiring skills and having the opportunity to use them. It is less universal and less automatic than you may assume.

The achievement of sexual freedom, I suggest, is threatened by half-truths, false expectations and subtle pressures to conform to a new set of standards imposed from outside. True freedom, surely, is the establishment of an individual sexual identity, the capacity to enjoy a wide range of relationships without evasion, deceit or illusion, the development of coherent values rid of the false myths of the present as well as of the past, and the capacity to grow as a caring, self-giving person.

The "letters" printed here were never, of course, mailed. It's unlikely that any parent would send actual letters like these. By the time any of our children had reached college age it would have been superfluous to exchange ideas about sex in writing. Unlike some people we have never believed that straightforward talk about sexual matters encourages teenagers to engage in irresponsible sex. Our children had no difficulty acquiring attitudes or information from us and they felt free to ask questions when they needed to. I have written for the benefit of those who have not had such open communication, and you might find that getting your parents to read this book would be a good way to open up discussion.

The letter format makes it clear that this is not a comprehensive source book for class use, but an attempt to discuss personal issues in a direct and practical way: there are several reliable textbooks to which you can turn for details and documentation. As far as is possible in a field that is continually developing, my information is up-to-date and I hope my academic respectability is established by my earlier books. Letters are not the place for footnotes. Books and articles quoted are generally identified by the author's name, and titles and publishers are given at the end of the book.

Most of the letters are addressed to a male and to a female student separately, because I think some points need to be stressed to one sex or the other; but I hope they will all be read by women and men alike. Each sex needs to be aware of the particular concerns and problems of the other. Occasionally it is important to note the specific person to whom a letter is addressed: for example in one letter to Paul the word "homosexual" is used for males only, although it can also, of course, be used for lesbians (as it is in the next letter to Jane).

Every fall I give a series of addresses to our freshmen and women, and their interest has encouraged me to share my ideas more widely. Last year one of them asked me by what authority I took it upon myself to talk to students about sexuality. I replied that I claim no decisive expertise. I have counseled many students about sexual problems, have read widely in the field and written several books on the subject. I have benefited from ongoing discussion with my wife, who is active in sex education and family planning, and who has made me aware of the validity of feminist complaints about sexual oppression. Although these letters are written in the first-person singular, they represent our joint attempt to share with you what we have said, or tried to say, to our children. Obviously this book is not a purely objective study: there are ideals and values implicit in it—though not, as you will find, the conventional ones. I do not expect you to agree with all I say; I shall be satisfied if I can encourage open and informed discussion and contribute to your achievement of true sexual freedom.

one:

FREEDOM

To Jane and Paul

Being away at college gives you freedom of many kinds—not least, of course, sexual freedom. In many ways the campus is a more sophisticated version of the *bukumatula* of the Trobriand Islands. The anthropologist Malinowski describes how, at puberty, boys and girls of this Melanesian tribe live together for some weeks in special houses owned by "some mature youth or young widower" (corresponding to your dean and resident advisors), to experiment sexually without any parental supervision. American students tend to be envious when they hear of this arrangement: they forget that the young Trobriand's brief opportunity for sexual experimentation is followed by an early marriage, strict prohibitions on extramarital affairs and very strong social barriers against divorce.

Actually, a modern American is much better off. You have four years pretty much free of external controls. You are spared the pressure-cooker atmosphere of the *bukumatula* and the unhappy prospect of having to choose one of your classmates as a husband or wife on graduation day. But you do have a wonderful opportunity to develop personal and sexual relationships. Despite the distorted image of campus sexuality frequently reflected in the media, you are not, of course, entering on a four-year orgy. The tendency among adults to picture coed dorm life as if it corresponded to the free-for-all of the *bukumatula* reflects, as one college chaplain put it, "more the frustrated yearnings of writers and readers than it does actual campus life." I'm not by any means denying that irresponsible and impersonal sexual behavior goes on, but the evidence is that most students want to develop serious relationships. The percentage of college men and women having their first experience of intercourse without any personal commitment is less, I suspect, than it was when I was in college. George Lower found that only two out of fifty women he interviewed at Edinboro State College in Pennsylvania favored permissiveness without affection. One of the women quoted in his study, who had engaged in coitus said, "For me the determining factor in premarital intercourse is the quality of the relationship. The relationship is far more important than anything else, no matter what it is! You must have things in common, and it is hard to separate a good relationship and a good sexual relationship. There is no division really." A male student commented in a discussion: "When intimacy becomes casual, and when your own personality and character and exposing yourself completely to somebody becomes casual, I think it could become very self-destructive. In fact, the more you expose a lot of yourself to a lot of people, the more you destroy yourself."

This doesn't mean, I think, that you and your friends are going to be without sexual problems. Unfortunately the freedom you enjoy is only partial, and it's threatened by restrictions you may not have thought of. Clearly you do have freedom from supervision. Most colleges have virtually abandoned attempts to control sexual behavior, provided it doesn't involve permanent cohabitation. Such control was never very effective, since you don't have to be in a college building between midnight and eight a.m. to be sexually active! Personally I welcome the abolition of parietals because it removes one possible source of immature behavior. One necessary element in teenage growth is the need to affirm one's independence as a person—and that means as a sexual person—by challenging parental authority.

That's why there is almost always conflict between children and even very liberal parents over hours for dating, entertaining members of the other sex in the bedroom and so on. For a college to extend the parental role in the inevitably less flexible form of rules and regulations is a mistaken attempt to perpetuate your childhood. The temptation to engage in thoughtless sexual activity simply to demonstrate your passage to adulthood is real when a school tries, however symbolically, to dictate behavior. The result is not a contribution to sexual freedom, because to have intercourse simply because it is forbidden by the dean is a reverse subordination to authority rather than a freely chosen step.

There's a second respect in which you enjoy a real freedom. Not only are you and your peers allowed virtually total freedom to engage in sexual activity; you are also rid of the atmosphere of suspicion about sexual intimacy that pervades our culture. It has been said that American society is "at the same time sex-centric and sex-rejecting." Sex is paraded blatantly for amusement, advertising and entertainment; but the same people who arouse the sexual instincts of the young to sell their products exhibit great anxiety if their children (especially their daughters) show signs of being sexually active. Even if parents have been supportive and understanding, the attitude of neighbors, teachers and churches has usually been condemnatory. One author has said that adults exhibit "an almost obscene obsession with the sexuality of the young . . . prompted by envious rancor and a bullying intention to interfere." At college you are able to explore sexuality relatively free of this oppressive ethos that condemns masturbation, makes a fetish out of premarital virginity and downgrades the values of sexual pleasure.

Don't exaggerate the degree of your freedom, however. I doubt if many of your friends (even those whose families have been as open as yours) are yet rid of the basically sex-rejecting influence of our culture. Intellectually you are

:7

free: psychologically and emotionally you will have to work at acquiring true liberty. You may have the opportunities of the *bukumatula* but you do not have the naïve innocence of Trobriand teenagers. Mary Calderone and Eric Johnson have recently emphasized how early we acquire our basic attitudes to sex. "By the time a child enters kindergarten," they write, "it has already had the most important and long-lasting sex education it can ever have." And unfortunately the early lessons are usually both negative and long-lasting. Your capacity for sexual fulfillment is likely to be complicated by feelings of guilt, however repressed, that make frank communication about sexual needs with a partner very difficult to achieve.

There's a third substantial freedom opened up by the mere fact of being in a new environment with entirely new people: freedom from the self you have established in your family and home community. The existentialists exaggerate the extent to which an individual can escape her or his nature and history. Indeed they deny that there is any "nature" that limits our freedom of action: we are what we do, they say, and the coward can choose at any time to be heroic. But whether we have an inborn nature or not, we certainly have our own history to cope with. The way we have acted in the past establishes patterns of expectation in ourselves and in our family and friends that are hard to break through. We can do it, perhaps, but our behavior is weighted towards conformity to our own past actions. At college you have an opportunity to start over that you may never have again. Nobody there knows much about you. How you present yourself in the next few weeks, how you relate to your roommate and the women and men in your dorm and your classes, how you behave at parties or on the playing field—these are at least largely open possibilities for you. But remember that within a few weeks you will have acquired a certain image there too, and that image in turn will be more difficult to modify next year or the year after. I hope this letter will be of some help as you face this exciting freedom to create your adult sexual self—which brings me to identify some of the *threats* to freedom you need to be aware of.

Most threatening of all is the conventional pattern of sexual interaction that our society imposes on its teenagers. While you will, I hope, find that college students ignore the traditional rituals of dating, the underlying attitudes abeorbed during high school are much more difficult to escape. From the early teens our culture gives confusing messages about sexuality. The external forms of romantic love and the emotional trappings of the dating game are encouraged, but honest encounter is made difficult and serious sexual involvement is frowned on. It is the competitiveness of sex, not its reality, that is fostered. Boys are encouraged to demonstrate their ability to pursue a girl but they are not expected to get her pregnant; at the same time they are neither informed adequately about birth control nor provided with the equipment to exercise it. Girls are encouraged to develop their capacities for teasing and titillation, but they are supposed to be sufficiently unaroused to discourage petting below the navel. The dynamics of sexuality are ignored so that when an adolescent couple find themselves engaging in intercourse, parental approval is irrationally withdrawn.

Adolescent relationships between the sexes all too often resemble a carefully planned and cunningly executed assault on the one hand, and a more or less persistent resistance in defense of virginity on the other. The girl is officially encouraged to entice the boy to the very gate of he citadel, while being at least discouraging when he attempts an entrance. She must defend herself from penetration while ensuring that the attacker's interest is not diverted nor his hope of conquest extinguished. The fact that the girl nowadays often gives in or even initiates the action does not affect the fact that male-female relations are antagonistic in style. The procedure is ritualized as an adversary relationship, so that honest communication, mutuality and friendship are excluded from sexual encunters. The sad persistence of this antagonism is reflected in a 1979 study that found that one out of every five students in a midwestern university reported experiencing violence in a courtship situation.

A second major threat to your freedom arises not from social convention but from the modern recognition of the power and importance of sex. Because we now acknowledge the existence of sexual needs from infancy and recognize their essential goodness, there's an impression that they must be satisfid at once. One student told me: "I think that sex is just one of the greatest pleasures of life, and that your body is ready for it and needs it at the age of puberty, and that when the body needs it you should accommodate the body's needs and your own desires." An analogy is frequently drawn between sex and eating; both, it is said, are responses to instinctual needs and it is as absurd (and as dangerous) to deny the one as it is to deny the other. A horror movie a few years back, *The Fear*, was promoted by an ad showing a man apparently raping a woman, with the caption "There are hungers no man can deny." It's a view widely touted on campus by some of the more vocal sexual athletes, often in order to justify their own promiscuity.

If we look a little more carefully at the analogy it proves to be far from persuasive, even if one accepts the primary assumption that all of us have an instinctual urge to sexual release. In the first place we do not applaud people who satisfy their hunger or sexual needs without some rational control. An alcoholic who drinks whenever he "needs" it, a member of a group on short rations who takes all she can get, or a man who satisfies his lust in rape are *not* acting acceptably. Secondly, we do not have to eat anything that is available; indeed abstention from thoroughly desirable foods is essential to the health of some people. Equally, abstinence from some forms of sexual release and the choice of other forms is entirely possible: a conscious decision, based on reasonable principles, to refrain from intercourse and to be satisfied temporarily with masturbation or petting may be

10:

thoroughly mature. What distinguishes the human animal is our capacity to control and direct our instincts in relation to long-term goals. Psychologists regard people who are governed by "irresistible impulses" as mentally sick, and it has been said that the brain is our most important sexual organ!

I suggest that the greater threat to sexual freedom today is not the denial of instinctual needs but the denial of human responsibility and choice. The psychologist Rollo May has called attention to a reverse "puritanism": "Sin used to mean giving in to one's sexual desires; it now means not having full sexual expression. Our contemporary puritan holds that it is immoral *not* to express your libido. . . . A woman used to be guilty if she went to bed with a man, now she feels vaguely guilty if after a certain number of dates she still refrains."

There's a final danger: it's what I call "the tyranny of statistics." In the past few years we have been bombarded with figures telling us what percentage of people do everything from masturbating to engaging in anal intercourse. This information undoubtedly contributes enormously to liberation from false fears and unnecessary guilt. But the research has two potential problems. In the first place, it tends to isolate the measurable aspects of sexuality—intercourse and orgasm—and to minimize the personal and emotional factors. And secondly, it is easily misinterpreted to imply that the majority practice is somehow healthy and the minority are a bunch of inhibited freaks. The authors of the major studies have been quite aware of the limitations of their findings, but popular interpretation all too often concludes that factual research has established the *desirable* norm when it has in fact established only the *statistical* average. The temptation to conform to the majority, especially in sexual behavior, is strong in our culture (despite our supposed admiration for the individual and the eccentric), and the campus is no exception. Surely freedom involves the development of your own distinctive sexual self—expressing your own inner being, establishing a set of coherent principles that you can live by with confidence, maintaining your individual integrity.

I know you don't want to be a mere cipher, just another item in a statistical majority. So be free to examine the alternatives and to make your decisions with critical insight and sensitivity. Be free to retain whatever you find to be truly human about the values we have shared with you; be free to reject whatever is spurious or thoughtless about the contemporary scene.

> *This above all: to thine own self be true,*
> *And it must follow, as the night the day,*
> *Thou canst not then be false to any man.*

two:

FALSE MYTHS

To Jane

I'm writing about some ideas that are popular among your peers, that claim to be based on facts—and are actually quite wrong or easily misleading. If you're to grow as an individual and not just follow the crowd, you need to recognize false assumptions when you meet them. Here are some false myths that you'll surely hear (the adjective is important: not all myths are false, and I'm speaking here of powerful and popular ideas that are in conflict with the facts).

First, many of your peers suppose that virginity is out of date. It's true, of course, that the number of women having intercourse in high school or college has increased steadily. But at least half of those who arrive on campus as freshmen have not had intercourse, and probably one out of four is still a virgin when she graduates from college. A Canadian study published in 1981 reported that one out of every three women students was an "adamant virgin," neither having experienced nor expecting to experience coitus during college. The interesting thing is that surveys show that most women *think* the number of college virgins is much smaller—because the majority are more vocal and like to represent themselves as the only mature people around. When one woman wrote in our women's center log, "Am I the only virgin on this campus? Should I do something about it?" five others anonymously added, "Me, too." Another wrote, "Don't do anything until you're ready!"

Because of the "tyranny of statistics" you'll be under great pressure to conform to the majority behavior. As one girl told Gloria Steinem, "It isn't just the boys who pressure you into bed, but it's the other girls. Not that they say anything, but just by being around them I feel like some kind of a nut." One sophomore confided to a counselor that her virginity was such a burden to her that "On a trip to Greece, I found any old Greek and did it so it wouldn't be an issue any more." You'll have to be strong to make up your own mind and not let others make it up for you.

You ought to keep these points in mind: If you act contrary to deeply held personal convictions about premarital intercourse you may suffer from guilt feelings that affect your future sexual adjustment if you marry. While abstaining from sex may be a sign of immaturity in some cases, it may be a sign of real personal strength and integrity to wait because you think the special intimacy and closeness of intercourse is best kept for the special commitment of marriage. Despite all the changes in sexual behavior many men attach less emotional significance to intercourse than women do, and you run the risk of investing more of your personal resources than you intend. Many a girl has said afterwards, "My virginity isn't something I wanted to preserve at all costs, but I sure wish I'd shared my first experience with someone who really cared for me rather than with a casual date or a fast talker."

A second widespread misconception is that petting is immature. For years, under the influence of Sigmund Freud, it was thought that petting, by allowing women sexual pleasure without intercourse, was liable to make it difficult for them to respond in intercourse. But the famous Kinsey reports helped to demolish this myth by showing a correlation between petting and *good* marital adjustment, and studies of female sexual response show that there is no biological distinction between orgasm in petting and in coitus. Petting can be a means of relieving sexual tension and of expressing intimacy, love and mutual caring without the danger of guilt feelings about intercourse or the threat of pregnancy. One sophomore commented: "I wish they wouldn't call it mutual masturbation . . . this is a two-people thing and I don't think it is anything to be ashamed of. We're in love and I feel we show our maturity by limiting ourselves to sexual behavior that can't hurt anyone." Another student told Gael Greene, "Girls keep telling me that what I have isn't really virginity anymore. You know that line—what's a hymen anyway, when you've done everything else in the book? But 'that' really is the big step. That's it . . . Petting is different. You can have all the warmth and affection and your virginity too." Some experts think women need to learn to respond physically in petting if they are to enjoy sex fully. Concentrating so much on intercourse and ignoring the pleasures open to us through the stimulation of the whole body is seen by therapists as a serious loss. In *The Hite Report* on female sexuality several women mentioned that they had stronger sexual feelings during "necking" or "making out" than they did later in intercourse. One wrote: "My best sexual experiences were all the heavy petting I did before I had intercourse at about nineteen; I used to do that for hours on end and fantasize afterwards for hours. It was the most beautiful, pleasureful thing in my life."

Thirdly, don't be taken in by the idea that any man who has an erection and doesn't have intercourse is going to suffer serious distress. Actually we now know that both sexes can experience discomfort (as well as disappointment) if extensive arousal doesn't lead to climax. But this doesn't mean that a woman has to engage in intimacy beyond what she feels is appropriate simply because the man wants intercourse. Nobody ever yet died of sexual starvation, and you can always help a man to have an orgasm during heavy petting. Because women have accepted the myth that men need intercourse they are often subject to what has been called "civilized rape" or "petty rape." Argument, persuasion and pressure are used to get a girl to go further than she wants in order to satisfy the man's sexual urge. You have the right to resist this subtle force as firmly as you would a violent attack on your body. You have a responsibility to yourself to decide when you engage in intercourse.

Another false myth is that pregnancy is no longer a problem. It's good, of course, that society can no longer force you to accept its standards by threatening you with pregnancy as the inevitable result of premarital sex. It's much better for you to have the freedom to develop your own moral standards and for your sexual behavior to be determined by positive ideals rather than by fears. But unfortunately the fact that pregnancy *can* be avoided has led to the impression that it *is* being avoided. That's just not true.

Education about birth control, as you well know, is woefully inadequate. Suitable contraceptives are still sometimes difficult to obtain without embarrassment. When you have them they are not all that simple to use effectively. Women sometimes count on the man to take the trouble to provide protection, even though the results of a mistake will be far less serious for him than for her. And it's now thought that a woman may unconsciously want it that way. "If I take the step of getting a contraceptive in advance," some seem to say to themselves, "I'll be making myself available, admitting that I'm sexy, and asking for trouble. If I'm carried away by passion on a beautiful evening or my boyfriend gets so worked up I can't say no—well anyway *I'm* not to blame." So the reality of one's sexuality is denied by a failure to plan contraception, and the result is that unwanted pregnancies are more likely to happen to women who don't intend to go all the way. It's not only those who are promiscuous who get caught; romantic idealists sometimes discover too late that they weren't able to control the situation.

I hope you won't get taken in by this myth and assume "it won't happen to me." Don't play Russian roulette with your life or that of another. According to a study done at Yale, about one out of every two pregnancies there occurs within the first five times of intercourse. So acknowledge your own

16:

sexuality (it's nothing to be ashamed of) and *either* abstain from intercourse or make as sure as you can that you take adequate precautions.

I'm sure I don't need to tell you that it's irresponsible to depend on abortion as a method of birth control. Although abortion, when it is legally available, is much less dangerous to your health than carrying a fetus to term, it's never a pleasant experience. It probably involves much less emotional trauma than bearing and bringing up an unwanted child, but it is inevitably a psychological strain. You may not think that a fetus is a person, but it is an elementary form of human life and some women who think they are free of objections to abortion find themselves feeling remorse after the event. You will remember that Toni had an abortion soon after her marriage because she was not ready for parenthood. Last week I met her with a two-month-old baby and she explained that, although they could hardly afford the loss of her income and didn't want to start a family yet, she just hadn't felt she could go through an abortion again.

Even though it is, or should be, a joint responsibility to provide contraception, I think it's very important for you to take your own precautions. Double safeguards are always in place here! I don't need to tell you (though you may need to tell some of your friends) that douching, having intercourse only during your period, avoiding orgasm or using *Norforms* are *not* effective birth control methods at all, though the first two may be better than nothing. The rhythm method, or any of the available techniques for establishing when ovulation takes place, are pretty difficult for a woman of college age to use. An instrument recently announced, which reliably monitors a woman's temperature changes using an electronic thermometer, may be a real breakthrough when it becomes available at a reasonable price. Most authorities don't think much of the reliability of spermicidal foam by itself (though it's excellent with a condom) or of suppositories like *Encare* and *Intercept*. Despite the anxieties of many college women, some form of the Pill with low estrogen is very safe at your age *provided you have regular medical check-ups.* A 1981 British study showed that the health risk of the Pill for women under 35 is negligible, even with extensive use. IUDs can be right for some people, but they present problems for most young women. With proper instruction and use, a diaphragm is highly effective. A collagen sponge or a progestin ring are alternatives some college students are using successfully. But whatever method you are comfortable with will be most effective.

Remember that the most reliable method of all is abstention from intercourse (though not necessarily from sex). I'm inclined to think that any man who's worth sleeping with should be prepared to accept one of the other ways of enjoying sexual satisfaction if you find all methods of contraception unacceptable.

Remember, too, that if the worst happens and you have unprotected intercourse or believe that your contraceptive device has failed for some reason, there are a number of "morning-after" procedures available. DES, if taken within seventy-two hours is pretty effective—though you shouldn't use it unless you are prepared to have an abortion if it proves ineffective. Some college health services recommend the insertion of a Copper 7 IUD within five days.

Finally, because scientific studies have officially confirmed (what many of us have known for some time) that women are as capable of sexual response as men, it is commonly supposed that they want *intercourse* as much as men. Masters and Johnson established that the female's capacity for intense and sustained physical pleasure is as great as or greater than the male's. But the media have often distorted their findings and interpreted them to mean that women want intercourse as much as men do and in the same circumstances. So when you suggest going to a movie instead of going to bed, or when you want to listen to the stereo rather than getting deeper into petting, your date has a new put-down ready to hand. "Oh, you just don't know yourself," he may say, "you're still hung up on those old Victorian inhibitions. Masters and Johnson have demonstrated that women can enjoy sex as much as men. Of course, if you're some kind of frigid freak, that's different. But if you're a real woman . . .''

The fact is that women are more dependent on the emotional circumstances of sexual activity than men are—though *The Hite Report on Male Sexuality* suggests that men are often more sensitive than they are able to admit. Whether this is due to cultural factors rather than to any innate qualities remains a matter of controversy. But even though some woman are nowadays apparently able to dissociate sex from affection, this is not true of the great majority of your age. So if you find that you are satisfied with kissing or hugging or general body contact when your male friend is ready for much more, don't think you have any reason to go beyond what is meaningful and pleasurable for you. If you do, the chances are you may feel inadequate for failing to respond and the guy may feel inadequate because he doesn't turn you on. One result of this myth of equal *readiness* as distinct from equal *capacity* could be that you break up a perfectly good personal relationship because you don't react just like a man.

Women's liberation surely includes freedom from having to model your sexual behavior on some pattern dictated by other people. *Our Bodies, Our Selves*, after all, calls the idea that women must be able to have sex at any time, without anxiety, under any conditions and with anyone, "alienating, inhuman, destructive and degrading." A woman in a discussion group put it like this: "Right now there is a lot of pressure on women to function well sexually. People feel it is unacceptable for a woman not to be able to have an orgasm because of all the literature and all the studies that are going on. That makes me nervous. That bothers me because it is in such contradiction to the way I was raised. It is like telling a girl to switch on all of a sudden. After not being allowed to, you are supposed to perform, and not just perform but to enjoy yourself. That is very hard for me." It's hard because it's unnecessary. I hope you can enjoy sex as a wonderful, joyous element in personal relationships without its ever becoming a burden.

three:
NEW COMMANDMENTS

To Paul

I must make it clear that in saying in my first letter that you're lucky to be free of the oppressive sexual ambiguity of our culture, and in urging you, in Hamlet's words, "This above all: to thine own self be true," I did *not* mean that sexual freedom involves indifference to common moral obligations. On the contrary, I think true freedom is inseparable from sensitivity to the fundamental ethical obligations we all share as human beings. So, without retracting anything I said before, I want to urge your serious consideration of what I will call "New Commandments" about sexuality. To call them commandments is a little dramatic—they could be called principles, or ideals, and none of them are orders that I or anyone else is about to enforce.

There's an important difference between moral duties we impose on ourselves and those that others impose on us. The process of reaching adulthood can be seen as the development of "inner commandments" to which responsible people are answerable not because they have been externally promulgated but because they have been embraced as rationally compelling to human consciousness. Studies in the development of moral reasoning suggest that we pass through at least three stages:

· A young child accepts the difference between right and wrong merely because he or she discovers that one kind of behavior has pleasurable results, while another is associated with pain or punishment.

· During adolescence rules are obeyed, even when doing so involves some personal loss or inconvenience, because the expectations and approval of the group (initially the family but later the community) become significant factors and sometimes outweigh the advantages of private pleasure. Rules are respected in the interest of a common good, even though the individual would act differently if he were on his own.

· At what has been called the "postconventional" stage, a moral standard is embraced and internalized so that it is felt to be binding in all circumstances. At this point the inner commandment may involve a person in conflict with the assumptions of society—as it did when many refused on moral grounds to fight in Vietnam.

Unfortunately a great many adults remain fixated at one of the childhood stages of development. Those who, merely for fear of social disapproval or divine punishment, govern their sexual behavior by submission to rules promulgated by a church or inscribed in the Bible are really moral dwarfs. Many students only *begin* to live by moral principles while they are in college, and all of us have a long way to go before we achieve ethical maturity and live consistently by coherent standards freely chosen. The external behavior of the moral adult may, of course, be very much like the behavior she or he was taught as a child: there's nothing necessarily immature about following the Ten Commandments or the teaching of Jesus *provided* you are doing so because you think them right and want, at least in your more responsible moments, to live that way as an expression of your own true self.

When I talk about new commandments, then, I'm merely formulating obligations that I believe you will recognize and assent to for yourself once I put them into words—though I find a surprising number of students haven't thought through the implications until I put them in the following way.

Don't Treat a Person as a Thing. To treat another person as a thing is to deny that individual's right to independent judgment and her or his equality with you as a free agent. A modern philosopher, Martin Buber, has pointed out how easy it is for us to treat people as *It*, as things, as instruments or means for our goals or interests, rather than as ends or beings with value in themselves and equal rights to independence. Instead of *meeting* others, says Buber, and encountering each person as a *you* to whom we can relate, by whom we may be changed, and from whom we will learn, we *use* them to serve our purposes, as tools for our advancement or convenience.

The application of this principle to sexual relationships is rather obvious. It means that it is irresponsible to use another person for my own physical satisfaction. Prostitution is an obvious example of people being treated as *It*. If someone says that prostitutes freely choose their trade, remind them of the economic pressures that force them to allow themselves to be treated as a mere assemblage of tissue, muscle and flesh for somebody's purely physical pleasure. And remember that psychologists believe that many female prostitutes are unconsciously getting back at the male sex—so that prostitution involves a double exploitation, two people each treating the other as a mere thing. The relatively small number of students who visit prostitutes find the experience, not surprisingly, pretty unsatisfying.

But technical prostitution is not the most common denial of the *you* in sexual behavior. The *Playboy* philosophy, for example, treats sex as "one of the ingredients in a total entertainment and service package for the young urban male," and encourages men to think that women are as pliable and disposable as the playmate of the month— conveniently packaged to be folded up in three sections when the next attraction comes along. A person is treated as a *thing* whenever she (or he) is pressured into sexual intimacy by false or exaggerated professions of love. To use the not very subtle blackmail "if you loved me, you'd go to bed with me" is to treat the other as a means, not as an end. To perpetuate the myth that the male, once aroused, will suffer "blue balls" unless he is relieved by intercourse is a form of coercion. To dismiss another person's hesitations as "Victorian" or "puritan" is to fail to take that person seriously as entitled to moral independence. To induce someone to engage in sexual activity by comparing them unfavorably with what is thought to be the "norm" is to reduce that person to a mere item in a statistical chart.

Men are not the only offenders. The "compulsive castrator" is by no means an unknown figure on campus. Margaret Drabble in *The Waterfall* gave a penetrating description of one such woman at Cambridge: "By the end of her first year Lucy was established as a *femme fatale* of a kind familiar to that small world—not cheerful, not even casual about her affections, but emotionally promiscuous, faithlessly intense, universally sincere. People fell in love with her to suffer, to share her exploratory sufferings, to share a share of her bed. She collected them. She liked their devotions, their pain. She thrived on them, grew strong on the arousing of unrequited passion. She sat there in her room in Newnham, a pale queen, and they gathered round her, seeking destruction; tenderly she wept over them, as she pulled off their wings, tenderly she drank coffee with them, and discussed their grief."

Violent rape is, of course, the ultimate *you*-denying aggressive sexual act. Few college students are responsible for blatant physical rape (though one out of four male students admits that he has used an element of force in sexual encounter). But, as Susan Brownmiller put it: "The man who presses his advantage, who uses his position of authority, who forces his attentions, who will not take no for an answer, who assumes that sexual access is his right-of-way and physical aggression his right-on expression of masculinity, conquest and power is no less of a rapist." Is it morally justifiable to use your charm or good looks or athletic prowess or academic reputation to seduce a woman, however "gently"? In an article in *The Village Voice* an anonymous author quoted the secret of Sanche de Gramont: "I discovered magic words that uncrossed legs, and magic potions and talismans. It never occurred to me to use force. The normal currency of courtship provided."

A great deal of pornography, as we are now beginning to realize, constitutes a violation of the integrity of women. And Meredith Tax in the following description brings into vivid focus an aspect of what it means for women to be reduced to objects: "A young woman is walking down a city street. She is excruciatingly aware of her appearance and of the reaction to it (imagined or real) of every person she meets. She walks through a group of construction workers who are eating lunch in a line along the pavement. Her stomach tightens with terror and revulsion; her face becomes contorted into a grimace of self-control and fake unawareness; her walk and carriage becomes stiff and dehumanized. No matter what they say to her, it will be unbearable. She knows that they will not physically assault her or hurt her. They will only do so metaphorically. What they will do is impinge on her. They will demand that her thoughts be focused on them. They will use her body with their eyes. They will evaluate her market price. They will comment on her defects, or compare them to those of other passersby. They will make her a participant in their fantasies without asking if she is willing. They will make her feel ridiculous, or grotesquely sexual, or hideously ugly. Above all they will make her feel like a thing."

Secondly, *don't conceive an unwanted child.* If your girl friend gets pregnant one of three things is likely to happen. You may get married, in which case the education of both of you may be fouled up, you will start a marriage with serious disadvantages, and eventually the baby may be blamed (however silently) for your problems. She may carry the fetus to term and either bring the baby up by herself or give it up for adoption: her education will be disrupted, both of you will probably suffer guilt and anxiety, and another child will be added to the millions who are denied the support of natural parents. If she decides to have an abortion she may go through a miserable and lonely experience and may have feelings of self-condemnation even if she has no religious convictions against abortion. When a student couple I counselled decided, reluctantly, on abortion, the woman felt that somehow the man had let her down doubly—first by impregnating her and then by expecting her to abort (even though she had fully shared both decisions)—and the marriage they had planned after graduation fell through.

In all the scenarios above it is the woman who suffers most: yet since the discovery of the Pill males have more and more expected her to be responsible for contraception. According to a recent report condom sales fell 100 million worldwide between 1961 and 1975, though happily there are indications that in the United States male readiness to accept responsibility is on the increase. Yet it is still true that the majority of young men say it is the woman's responsibility—while paradoxically they not infrequently condemn a woman who takes precautions before intercourse. It seems to me that since the woman has most to lose by an unwanted pregnancy the only human or moral principle is for the man to be *more* responsible for contraception than she is—rather than saying, as some do, "She'll have to cope if anything goes wrong, so let her take the precautions." That's hardly treating her as a *you!* Add to this the fact that the male is probably more likely to press for intercourse and the woman is much less likely to enjoy an orgasm and find the experience in itself sexually satisfying, and the case for primary male responsibility is surely overwhelming.

This is not the place, even if it were necessary, to give you detailed information about birth control. Until there's a practicable male pill (not expected before 1990 at the very earliest), a good condom offers a high level of protection.

:25

Best of all, use a spermicidal foam like *Emko* or *Delfen* as well. And incidentally there's absolutely no reason why *you* shouldn't buy this in a drugstore when you get condoms, rather than expecting her to do so!

There are two objections to using a condom that I hear from students. Some (though not all) complain that it reduces sensation and spoils the physical pleasure. That seems to me a very small price to pay for security against pregnancy, and I have little patience with those who raise the objection and expect to be regarded as serious moral agents. (Condoms made of cecum which are a little more expensive are said to allow more sensation.)

A second objection is that putting on a condom introduces an unacceptable, unaesthetic mechanical action that interrupts the romantic joy of making love. Some men have difficulty having or maintaining an erection with a condom. If you have such a problem I suggest you let your partner put the condom on and make it part of mutual foreplay. I will go further and ask whether, if your friendship is not intimate or open enough to make this possible, you ought to be having intercourse at all? Any type of birth control depends for its effectiveness on careful, planned application. If you are embarrassed or uncomfortable with your partner so that you can't discuss what method you are using, you probably won't be properly protected. If either of you is engaging in the activity because of some pressure ("I didn't really want to but it seemed to matter so much to him" or "I felt she expected me to play the aggressive male role") your chances of disaster are considerable. If you're both overwhelmed by a romantic evening, or by pot or alcohol, or you're both horny on a casual date, you're simply being irresponsible if you go all the way without protection. Remember that *abstention* from intercourse is the only fully effective method of birth control (and that *doesn't* mean abstention from sex). Free yourself from the absurd myth that scoring is all that counts. Treat her as a person and not as a bull's-eye, and you'll discover that petting to orgasm or oral sex can be profoundly eatisfying without the dangers of coitus.

My third "commandment" can be dealt with quite briefly. *Don't extend the VD epidemic.* This may seem irrelevant to you, but venereal diseases are far from unknown among college students, although they are very hesitant to admit it. Gonorrhea, as you surely know, is in epidemic proportions throughout the country; two out of every three cases *reported* occur among the 15–24 age group—that means well over two million people in the USA today. Happily the incidence of venereal diseases among college students is relatively low, but it goes without saying that anyone who has symptoms or any reason to think he or she is infected has a moral responsibility not to share that condition with a sexual partner. Remember that anyone who engages in intercourse with another person who has had several sexual encounters, is at risk. You not only have the prospect of discomfort and possibly serious illness for yourself: you have the responsibility of infecting an innocent partner whom you profess, probably, to "love."

The most effective safeguard, of course, is to avoid intercourse or oral sex unless you and your partner have not slept with anyone else. Other activities such as petting are less likely to spread these diseases. The careful use of a condom offers significant protection. But remember that people who are far from promiscuous may have VD today, and that many (particularly women) are carriers without symptoms. Remember too that venereal diseases, when professionally treated early, are almost always curable, but if unattended can have serious long-term consequences. A doctor or clinic will *not* treat you as a social outcast and your name will *not* be reported to your parents, or to your sexual contacts. The only way to reduce the incidence of VD and the suffering caused is through honest, unembarrassed recognition of the problem as a medical issue and a responsible effort not to extend the epidemic further.

Obviously this third commandment has implications similar to the first two—abstain from casual, impersonal sex. A recent textbook concludes a thorough discussion of VD with these words: "It is a paradox that people who engage in the physical intimacy of a sexual relationship are unable to communicate about the ramifications of the relationship. If feelings of guilt and shame over having a sexual relationship prevent people from getting good medical care, then some thought has to be given to how they are using their sexuality."

I don't want this letter to leave you with the impression that I think all sexual activity has to involve heavy discussion. Your generation is fortunate in being able to enjoy sex more freely than mine, and I certainly don't want to make it less fun. The best sex is carefree and abandoned, and when you and a partner have well-founded confidence in each other anxiety can be put aside. But unfortunately it's easy to convince ourselves that we are engaging in harmless play when we are in fact doing psychological damage or emotional harm. Such behavior should, surely, make us feel guilty—not, as in the past, simply because we are engaging in sex, but because we are acting in some way that is irresponsible or inhumane.

I find myself unsure how often chance sexual interludes are truly fulfilling. Provided the people involved are honest with each other and no unwanted pregnancy or infection results, they can certainly be very satisfying. Lorna and Philip Sarrel, who run the remarkably successful educational and counseling program at Yale, believe that recreational sex is "an important, perhaps indispensable part of human experience" with the potential to enhance "sexual unfolding" (the last phrase, which I like a great deal, is the title of their book). On the other hand they also remind us that: "Casual sex is risky. But it can be worth the risk. Risky or not, it happens a lot. People can grow emotionally as a result. When it is natural and easy, it can be a good time. It can also be a time of feeling used and losing self-esteem. It can be a setup for failure." What the outcome is depends, I suspect, a great deal on the sexual maturity of those involved. I hope that what I've said will help you to be more aware of the complexities of all your relationships, without putting a damper on your enjoyment of them.

four:
HUMAN NATURE

To Jane

I'm glad to know you're enrolling in a course in sociobiology. It's clear that the study of animal social groups and the behavioral adaptations that have been advantageous in the evolutionary process can tell us a good deal about the human situation. The more we know about the instinctual equipment we start with, the better chance we have of developing adequate social and personal means of survival. On the other hand, it does seem to me that the sociobiologists, in their enthusiasm for tracing what we have in common with other species, tend to downplay the distinctive freedom of humankind and to minimize the capacity of reason to direct instinct. It is this, of course, that has made the book you mention, *The Evolution of Human Sexuality*, so controversial. If Donald Symons is right and the male desire for multiple partners has been advantageous, while females have survived better when they have been more selective, does it not follow that the "double standard" for sexual behavior is in our genes? Are we not just acting naturally when men are promiscuous and women monogamous?

It's not that simple. Indeed, the definition of what is natural is one of the most difficult to decide. One possible use is to equate it with whatever a human person is capable of doing. In this sense, virtually any known sexual behavior is natural. The only unnatural acts would be physically impossible—like having intercourse with yourself. The condition of a person with female chromosomes (XX) but with male external genitals might, in this usage, be termed unnatural; yet that seems both unfair and inappropriate since it is certainly nature and not human intervention that has produced the anomaly. On the other hand rape, necrophilia and pederasty would have to be considered natural, and that doesn't make sense.

A very common usage is to equate the natural with the conventional. Each society tends to identify whatever sexual behavior is acceptable in its group or tribe or culture with the natural. In this way the isolation of deviants or eccentrics is given some kind of moral justification, and enemies are often said to engage in unnatural sexual practices, thus adding to the reasons for eliminating them. Anthropologists have shown us how inadequate this usage is. Margaret Mead made us familiar with societies in which men are maternal and nurturing, in which women are aggressive and insensitive, and in which males engage in dancing and art while females do the heavy work. I have just read a review of a book describing a Papuan tribe in which all males from childhood through late adolescence are required to engage in homosexual fellatio, ingesting the semen of mature males in order (it is thought) to acquire the strength necessary to succeed in warfare. This pattern is thought absolutely natural by the Sambian people. So there's nothing peculiarly natural about our very different conventions.

The Catholic Church has for centuries claimed that it can be shown rationally that the traditional standards of Western culture are rooted in nature in a way that others are not. This assumption is reflected in the religious (and frequently legal) condemnation of certain types of sexual behavior as unnatural—e.g., masturbation, homosexual acts, anal intercourse, and most methods of contraception. The argument, based on Stoic and Aristotelian ideas, is that the sexual organs have specific functions for which nature has designed them (and for which nonhuman animals use them) so that to use them for other purposes or to interfere with their biological function is unnatural. By a remarkable and happy coincidence Western cultural expectations coincide, it is claimed, with the practices of nature!

There are three fundamental difficulties with this claim. In the first place animals, including primates in the wild, frequently engage (contrary to medieval belief) in masturbation and homosexual acts. In the second place, it is difficult to see how it can be unnatural to use a condom, for example, to avoid conception, but natural to use a thermometer to establish the time of ovulation for exactly the same purpose. Finally, by identifying the natural with the biological function, Catholic thought has had the effect of defining human sexual relationships in physiological terms and ignoring the personal and emotional significance of sex. Intercourse clearly has a significance for humans that is much broader than its reproductive function. We need a concept of the natural that does justice to the uniqueness and complexity of *human* sexuality.

I'm not sure that modern usage offers us that, if "doing what comes naturally" means "doing what instinct and physical need demand." But that is what some ethologists and sociobiologists seem to say. If humans are merely "naked apes," in Desmond Morris's phrase, the implication seems to be that instinctual impulses control human behavior. But the more careful students of animal behavior recognize that this is a gross oversimplification.

The whole point of Konrad Lorenz's book *On Aggression* was to argue that the human race can only survive if we acknowledge the reality of our animal inheritance *and take the necessary rational steps to find alternative ways* of expressing our aggressive instincts. He has explicitly repudiated the view that instinctual forces are irresistible. For Lorenz "the greatest gift of all, rational responsible morality" gives humans the power to control instinct, and he has warned that to take "the theoreticians of complete sexual promiscuity" at their word would involve enormous damage to human culture. Even Edward O. Wilson, the father of sociobiology, who denies the existence, or at least the relevance, of any properties "that cannot be translated into neurons, circuits, or any other physical units," recognizes that we are "free and responsible persons" in a fundamental sense. Symons himself, in a recent interview, acknowledged that sociobiology "tells us nothing about whether or not we are free to act on our impulses" and affirmed that his theories "have absolutely nothing to do with right and wrong and no implications for what one ought to do."

Mary Midgley, a British philosopher, has written a book on this subject, *Beast and Man*, that I wish every student enrolled in a course on sociobiology would read. She makes the important point that discussion of the "nature/nurture" issue has been clouded by the false assumption that it involves a choice *between* instinctual and learned behavior: "This polarization seems much like holding that the quality of food is determined *either* by what it is like when you buy it *or* by how you cook it." What the recent intensive study of animal behavior has shown is that other animals are less antisocial, violent, and irrational than human pride has been prepared to admit, and that we are much more like them than the Western philosophical and religious tradition has allowed. Midgley puts it well: "Natural feelings like our strong and special affection for our children are not just loose facts about us; they are the sort of thing that constitutes our central good. Moral surgeons who want to cut them out because of their dangers [she quotes Plato's *Republic* as an example] misconceive their function. We are simply not in a position to replace them with something else which will not be worse. The choice we have is a choice between better and worse ways of expressing them. There is no such choice as dropping them altogether." But because our instincts are, in Midgley's phrase, "open . . . programs with a gap," they have to be integrated with the distinctively developed human capacities for learning, speech and choice. Humans are more free than other species, and that freedom is as much part of human nature as the characteristics we share with other animals. It is unnatural to repress our instincts or to deny their proper part in human life. It is equally unnatural to allow them to determine our behavior or to disclaim moral responsibility for our actions.

Much of our sexual behavior is shared with other animal species—including the urge of the majority towards intercourse and reproduction (or, to be precise, the urge of males to have orgasm and ejaculate and the biological readiness of females to allow them, *when they learn*, to copulate at times of fertility). Without this capacity we would not have survived as a species. But in humans, sexuality has become much more important and much more complicated. We enjoy sex apart from procreation, human female response is not limited to an estrus cycle and human females are apparently unique in experiencing orgasm under natural conditions. Sex has social and interpersonal meanings for us far beyond the range of any other species. The uniqueness of human self-consciousness is inseparable from sexual identity—as well as its problems. The British psychiatrist Anthony Storr has said that "sex is so important, so pervasive, and so intimately connected with every aspect of personality that it cannot be separated from the person as a whole without impoverishing even superficial relationships . . . the kind of contact which we make with each other in ordinary social exchanges at a superficial level is determined by the capacity we possess for making deeply intimate relationships."

When moralists warn people that absorption in sexual activity is "descending to the level of the beasts," they are talking sheer nonsense: other animals spend far less time engaging in sex than we do. What is less than human is not spending a lot of time in sexual encounter but rushing through it, isolating it from the complex grid of personal and social meanings it has acquired. Rape, for example, is the ultimately unnatural sexual act for humans because in rape sex is used not as a means of personal interaction but as an instrument of aggression.

I am *not* saying that sex is only good when it serves serious social and personal ends, or that sex-as-fun ("ludic sex," as one writer has called it) is unnatural or subhuman. What I am arguing is that "doing what comes naturally" cannot, for human beings, be equated with the satisfaction of instinctual needs any more than it can be equated with pure rationality or spirituality. What is distinctive to *human* nature is the integration of sex and personal relationships. We should surely most of the time aim at what the psychologist Abraham Maslow called "the farther reaches of human nature." The following criteria suggested by Lester Kirkendall, a leading sex educator, seem to me to set forth as well as anything what is most human in sexual behavior: "The moral decision will be the one which works toward the creation of trust, confidence, and integrity in relationships. It should increase the capacity of individuals to cooperate, and enhance the sense of self-respect in the individual. Acts which create distrust, suspicion, and misunderstanding, which build barriers and destroy integrity, are immoral. They decrease the individual's sense of self-respect, and rather than produce capacity to work together they separate people and break down the capacity for communication."

Such a definition may help us to identify the "unnatural" too. We can escape from the arbitrariness of conventional categories that condemn sexual behavior as unnatural simply because it is the preference of a minority, because it does not serve reproduction, or because it is thought unaesthetic or bizarre. We can regard as natural any behavior human ingenuity can devise, provided that it does not threaten a person's psychic health or interfere with interpersonal growth. Any activity that is forced on another person, that embarrasses a partner, that becomes compulsive, or that isolates an individual from other people will be regarded as unnatural.

By this test some homosexual behavior would be natural and some heterosexual behavior would be unnatural. Masturbation would be accepted as healthy unless it became obsessive, or was a substitute for all interpersonal sex. Oral sex or anal intercourse would sometimes be thought natural and sometimes not. Fetishism or transvestism, provided they did not involve compulsions that interfered with effective operation as a member of society, might sometimes be accepted. Sado-masochism, provided it involved no real bodily harm, would be within the range of normality. As Midgley says, "That consenting adults should bite each other in bed is in all senses natural; that school teachers should bully children for their sexual gratification is not." Voyeurism might be regarded as natural provided it did not replace all sexual relationships, or infringe on the sensibility of the person observed. On the other hand I cannot imagine any circumstances in which rape (however subtle), exhibitionism, or child molestation could be conceived as natural. In the final analysis the person or persons concerned, or perhaps an experienced counselor, would have to make the judgment in doubtful cases. But at least a rational criterion based on an understanding of *human* sexuality would be applied.

five:

FREE MEN

To Paul

I share your concern over the attitude of some of your peers towards women. What I hear from women, and occasionally from men, tells me that in groups of their own sex male students perpetuate a lot of immature adolescent antagonism. Whether they privately live up to the expectation that they will "score" or "screw" regularly is uncertain. Apparently you live in an atmosphere of goal-oriented pressure that discourages sensitivity. Obviously these men think they are supremely free—young lords of creation able to satisfy their sexual appetites at whim and sought after by eager, beautiful women. Of course it's not really like that now—it never was quite that easy—and their freedom is a delusion. Despite their apparent self-confidence they are in captivity: captivity to ignorance, to anxiety and to an impoverished cultural tradition.

People go to college to learn, and have no difficulty in admitting their limited knowledge of any subject in the academic curriculum. But sex is one object on which everyone is a self-proclaimed authority: publicly to admit ignorance in this field is to accept humiliation, at least among males. Perhaps it's the reverse side of the unfortunate fact that when they were growing up their parents encouraged curiosity and offered information in any field *except* sex! But the actual degree of ignorance and misinformation, to judge from initial tests administered to those enrolled in courses in sexuality, is phenomenal. Dr. Arnold Werner, who writes a column called "The Doctor's Bag" for students at Michigan State and elsewhere, reports an almost unbelievable confusion among students over the most elementary matters. Some think that pregnancy can be avoided if the woman does not have an orgasm, or if she has intercourse daily, or by drinking alcohol "to get the sperm drunk before intercourse." Many men believe there is a "normal" size for the penis and that sexual satisfaction depends on being within the precise limits. Male masturbation is thought, quite contrary to Kinsey's findings, to have a negative effect on intercourse or to be a purely adolescent practice. Letters about venereal disease are often unsigned, indicating continued embarrassment about the subject. Some women are ignorant about the hymen (very few are aware that occasionally a minor surgical operation is required to break it) and others worry that ingesting semen is dangerous to health.

A few years ago two anxious readers of *Playboy* wrote in distress to say that they had not yet experienced intercourse and feared for their sexual health. To which the omniscient *Playboy* Advisor replied, correctly: "Abstinence, as such, is neither good nor bad for the health. What does affect the individual's well being are the circumstances of, and the motivations for, his abstention. Kinsey points out that men who are physically incapacitated, natively low in sex drive, sexually unawakened in their early years or separated from their usual sources of sexual stimulation can abstain indefinitely without appreciable harm. Even when these conditions do not prevail, if the motivation for abstention is conscious and rational, no harm will be done."

Even more disturbing, and self-defeating, is the abysmal ignorance of the fundamentals of female anatomy and of the way to arouse a woman sexually and satisfy her needs. Shere Hite found recently that the great majority of men still suppose that all women can easily enjoy orgasm merely through stimulation by the penis in coitus, even though it is now known that this is true only of a minority.

The result of this captivity to ignorance is a second, more serious bondage to anxiety. Because men suppose, quite wrongly, that if they are sexually normal their partner should be able to come to orgasm during intercourse, the failure to help to bring this about becomes a source of self-doubt that can lead to difficulty in attaining erection and thus perpetuate a vicious cycle. The fact is that two out of every three women (perhaps a higher percentage among inexperienced women of college age) need careful, sensitive manual stimulation of the clitoral area either before, during or after coitus if they are to reach orgasm. The male who is ignorant of this fact but properly concerned that sexual fulfillment be shared by his partner often feels responsible for her lack of orgasm. Hite quoted these typical comments: "I'd feel that I should have done something more, such as a longer foreplay." "If the person I am with would not orgasm, I'd feel inadequate, like I wasn't enough of a man for her or something. It'd put a big shattering strain on my confidence." "I feel inadequate. Sometimes I wonder just how good a sex partner I am."

Many men suppose that the inability to sustain an erection long enough to "bring her to orgasm" constitutes impotence, or that ejaculating before the partner has reached her climax constitutes premature ejaculation. "The only time I am anxious that I am not '*man* enough' . . . is when I have inexplicably lost my hard-on and cannot continue. What the hell happened? I ask myself. How come? How delicately am I balanced, anyway? It is frustrating and embarrassing. It makes me feel like I am a little helpless boy, guilty usually, I feel ashamed," one man wrote to Hite. But such fears are almost always unfounded. The inability to have an erection at all is very uncommon and may be due to pathology; occasional difficulty with erection is experienced by two out of every three men. Premature ejaculation strictly means ejaculation immediately on arousal, or immediately on vaginal penetration. It's a condition not uncommon in young men: a first attempt at intercourse is often frustrated for this reason. It normally ceases to be a problem with experience and can usually be controlled by simple techniques if it persists in manhood. But most students are not suffering from either problem. Their problem arises from setting an unattainable goal—stimulation of a partner to orgasm with the penis. When they ejaculate before the woman has an orgasm or, after a long period of vaginal penetration, fail to produce the expected result, they become anxious about their failure and out of fear of a likely repetition may have difficulty with erection on the next occasion. The resolution of the dilemma lies in abandoning the mistaken idea that female orgasm is usually brought about by a penis, or indeed the idea that pleasure is something that a man has to accomplish for or give to a woman.

The fact is that the sexual big shots on campus are far less mature and self-assured than they would like you to think. Rollo May says that "the less mature the person, the more the simply physiological gratification itself carries the value and the less difference is made by *who* gives the gratification." One experienced campus psychiatrist reported that "while the alienated student seems to be leading a sexually stimulating life, he frequently complains that it is unsatisfying and meaningless. Intimacy, self-respect, and even orgasm are usually lacking." And another study of student sexual behavior concluded that "those seniors who seemed to be going a long way in terms of personality development had a history of rather slow and gradual unfolding of sexual interests and behavior."

The sad thing is that the fundamentally goal-oriented assumptions with which some of your friends approach sex have been imposed on them by our culture rather than freely chosen. They are still captive to the pattern of interaction with women that the dating game introduced them to. I tried in an earlier letter to show how basically antagonistic and adversary-like these rituals are. But they are prepared for and supported by a process of conditioning that begins in the cradle and permeates every aspect of "patriarchal society."

Even those who eventually achieve independence often have a great deal of difficulty during the years at college in dissociating themselves from the subtle ideology by which they have been formed. Assumptions of masculine superiority are so deeply imbedded in our corporate psyche—both in men and in women—that most students still accept their traditional roles even when they don't make them particularly happy. Hite puts the point strongly but, I think, accurately: "If it were simply a problem of reason and understanding, sexual problems between men and women would have been settled long ago. Instead, men (and, especially in the past, women, for reasons of their own) tenaciously cling to the dominant view of what sexuality is/should be, according to the overall cultural ideology—because this ideology is stronger than facts or reality. Men believe that this ideology, which gives them power, gives them the best of all possible worlds and that therefore they have a vested interest in maintaining things the way they are, and so resist change."

These attitudes deeply affect relationships between men and women from childhood to adulthood. Boys are taught, while being superficially respectful of girls and women, at all costs not to be *like* them. By example as much as by word, they learn that males are not expected to show emotion or to cry when they are hurt; it is their role to take charge and be successful in any kind of competition or sport; it is inconsistent with masculinity to need or give physical affection. I remember being vividly reminded of this tradition a few years ago when the seven-year-old son of a Vietnam veteran, on meeting his father on return from a POW camp, went up to him and solemnly shook his hand. Typical expressions of the problem received by Hite were: "Men should not hurt, cry, openly display affection or react to emotion in another. I feel embarrassed when someone shows strong or tender emotions. I feel embarrassed for him." "We have been taught it is the woman who should have and show her feelings and it is unmanly for us to do the same." "My friends in high school called another guy a sissy when he said he was afraid to ask his girl to go all the way. I hadn't either but I didn't say anything. The idea was that we were all men because we could brazen our way through any girl's defenses—make the tackle and complete the pass, so to speak. What she felt didn't matter (what we felt either, as far as that goes)—so long as we scored. We listened to these stories from each other, secure in our knowledge that we were being men—the others were sissies." Scoring, of course, meant intercourse and intercourse was what sex was about: anything less than that counted for nothing. If you were stopped or faltered at the five-yard line you'd failed!

This early training is very effective—and tragically restrictive. Not only does it define male sexual behavior in a narrowly rigid fashion: *it defines it in terms that are inevitably at cross purposes with what we know about female sexual needs*. For all too many of your peers there are four virtually unconscious principles operating that make sexual relationships of true equality impossible: first, intercourse is what really counts; second, intercourse is a symbolic expression of male superiority; third, whatever goes on before intercourse is strictly foreplay, perhaps a necessary preliminary, but nothing more; fourth, intercourse is the only permissible context for physical expressions of affection or intimacy.

Perhaps the most troubling fact to emerge from Hite's study is that a fifth principle operates in a significant number of men—dislike of, contempt for and hidden but deep anger against women, including mothers and wives. Sometimes, paradoxically, this arises from women's perceived weakness and their acceptance of the subordinate position that men have imposed on them—combined with a suspicion that women have a dangerous power to manipulate men. In other words, they are damned if they allow men to dominate them and damned if they attempt to redress the situation! Another common complaint is that men are expected to carry the burdens of economic responsibility and sexual initiative, while women (especially in the liberation movement) show

42:

no appreciation for what they owe the other sex. Once again, women are caught either way: if they accept the pattern of male leadership they are accused of putting an unfair onus on men, and if they begin to establish their own independence they are blamed for ingratitude for male generosity.

Many male students will acknowledge the existence of this one-sided cultural bias, but they respond by asking, "What can we do about it? It's inherent in our nature, part of our genetic structure, or at least so deeply established in our lifestyle that it can't be changed." This is not the place to get into that extremely complex and controversial issue in detail. There are some who regard male dominance as purely learned. Sociobiologists like Donald Symons attribute the differences to genetic traits necessary to evolutionary survival. The evidence of predisposing prenatal hormonal factors seem to be rather strong. Eleanor Maccoby, who did the most thorough survey of the literature and concluded that aggressiveness is the only universal characteristic distinguishing the male, believes that both biological and social causes play a part. I suspect that we males are affected by the fact that we all start life totally dependent (in the womb, if not at birth) on a woman and that she is the first both to give and to deny us pleasure. There is often a lingering, repressed guilt over our infantile oedipal desire for our mother and an unconscious resentment of her rejection of that desire. As a sex we probably retain hidden feelings of jealousy and fear of creatures who can reproduce by themselves (as early man, lacking understanding of impregnation, supposed). Primitive taboos about menstrual blood, the sign of the female's capacity to bleed without suffering harm or death, are far from eliminated from our psyche.

These are real and fascinating facts of which we must take account, but all together they surely provide no justification for the perpetuation of male dominance in our social or sexual lives. What distinguishes *humans* is our capacity to outgrow and increasingly control these forces that oppress women or deny them sexual equality and fulfillment. It may be difficult to change our behavior; it may require therapy to resolve oedipal conflicts; it may be impossible or undesirable to eliminate all sex-role distinctions. But it is certainly not beyond our capacity to modify established inequalities, and the campus is surely where such changes should begin—if, that is, there is anything in our claim that colleges are places where people *learn*. The freedom you seek must surely include freedom from the oppressive concept of male sexuality by which all of us men are affected. Remember that those who maintain a prison are restricted and bound by their own captives!

There are signs that progress is being made. According to *The Hite Report on Male Sexuality*, a significant number of men are profoundly dissatisfied with their traditional role: "I don't know. I know what I am told makes a man, but I am not sure at all that those are real. In men, I admire openness, sensitivity, strength of character, kindness, all of them the same things that I admire in anyone, male or female. I am proud of my effort to redefine for myself what masculinity, or perhaps better what humanity is, without listening to and buying all the stuff I have been told by society over the years." The macho ideal was rejected as artificial and insecure by most of Hite's respondents: " 'Macho' is a state of mind, consisting of insensitivity, competitiveness, conceit, and self-worship, whereas masculinity is more subtle, secure, and understated." More and more men reject the idea that it is typically masculine to separate sex and emotional involvement. Many of them say that physical and psychological closeness is more important in intercourse than orgasm itself.

A second straw in the wind is that *The Playboy Report on American Men*, published in 1980, found that the quality most commonly sought in an ideal lover (whether among "traditionalists" or "innovators") was "someone to be totally open and honest with." And the innovators—those probably representing the trend of the future—compared to the

44:

traditionalists, down-played the importance of such qualities as "accepting you just as you are," "sensitive to your needs" and "loyal to you, right or wrong." There is at least a trend towards accepting women as equals.

Finally, there have been far-reaching changes in the way men perceive themselves and the way they act. Gloria Steinem in *Ms* magazine (June, 1981) drew attention to the following areas of change:

> By 1978, fewer than 30 percent of Americans disapproved of 'a married woman earning money if she has a husband capable of supporting her.' In 1938, the disapproval rate was more than 75 percent.

> By 1980, a majority of Americans agreed that 'both sexes have responsibilities to care for small children.' In 1970, agreement had been only about 30 percent, a big change in a decade.

> For the first time in history, a majority now rejects the double-standard idea that a woman should be a virgin when she marries, or that it's more excusable for a husband to have affairs.

> By 1980, nearly 80 percent of Americans were willing to vote for a woman President. In 1937 only about 30 percent would have agreed.

> At the beginning of the 1970s, only a 42 percent minority of Americans wanted to strengthen women's status in society. By the end of the decade, a 64 percent majority agreed.

I think there's hope for us, and perhaps for the human race if this new image of masculinity permeates the political scene and delivers us from the disasters of a nationalistic macho foreign policy.

six:
FREE WOMEN

To Jane

Your problem with Jim is *far* from uncommon! Among the
women who come to talk with me about their sexual
relationships, the majority are troubled by the fact that
they feel pressured into greater intimacy—specifically,
intercourse—than they are ready for. They usually like the
guy a great deal, though they often don't quite want to say
they "love" him. They enjoy being with him, talking, doing
things together, kissing and petting. They want to continue
the relationship and allow it to develop, often feeling that it
might lead to full sexual intimacy; but they aren't ready for
intercourse yet and don't feel he should expect it of them. As
in your case, the man makes a big thing of how important it
is to *him*, how it will draw them closer. He asks why she can't
sleep with him for his sake, even if she isn't all that keen.
And he lays a guilt trip on her because, he says, he obviously
can't mean very much to her if she's unready to share her
body. So women come to me in deep distress because they
sincerely feel affection for a man, don't want to hurt him,
and yet aren't able to go all the way without giving up
something of their own integrity and independence. The
result is that sex, for some women of your age, is becoming a
burden and a bore.

One of my students who has been off campus this year
wrote last week in this vein: "Last year I went through a
typical sophomore slump. I hated men and I let myself get

sucked into oppressive situations and relationships . . . My relationship with Tom came to an end in February, but I feel really good about it. He said he was 'in love' with me but had to have me as his girl or *nothing*—no friendship or anything. Consequently we don't have much of a friendship anymore. It's not my style at all, but neither was having intercourse after a month's relationship." She goes on to write about discussions she's had with other women who feel "very insecure about their own sexuality." "They all feared relationships with men," she says, "because the pressure to have sex (and eventually intercourse) with them was so great. None of them had much in the way of relationships and very little sex. The infuriating thing about it is that they feel as though they are weird and odd for not having had much sex. . . . Some of my friends who do have intense sexual relationships don't enjoy it. My roommate this semester *hates* sex and yet she does it a lot. Now tell me, does that make sense?"

My advice to women in this kind of situation is what I've said to you often in the past: you must make up your mind whether you have value as a person in your own right, or whether you derive value from men. Our society is so structured that you have been brought up to think of yourself as significant only if you are the girl-friend or lover or wife of some male. Your role in life, you learn from an early age, is to provide support for males and to contribute to their pleasure. Of course, women's liberation has begun to change this and I hope your mother and I have been successful in helping you to affirm your own independent identity. But it's very difficult when you meet a man you really like and want to have as a friend and perhaps as a lover and he's still caught up in the typical male role. I suspect that Jim is *in principle* all for women's freedom and equality, otherwise I doubt if you'd like him as much as you do. But it's a terrible shock to a man when someone he loves isn't prepared to go along with his idea about a sexual relationship. Unfortunately I don't see any easy way out. Either you compromise your own integrity and accept second-class citizenship *or* you continue to explain to him as patiently and gently as you can that you have a responsibility to yourself to determine how far you want to go sexually. Stress that saying no at this juncture is no rejection of him, nor is it necessarily saying that you will never have intercourse with him.

The fact is that women's liberation has a long way to go in the area of sexuality—far further, indeed, than in other respects. The last bastion we men are about to surrender is the privilege of determining how and when our sexual needs are satisfied, and we've been remarkably successful in turning the new understanding of female sexuality to our own convenience. The double standard is alive and well in America. Women's sexual liberation as interpreted by men turns out to mean freedom to enjoy sex the way men do, or freedom to satisfy male desires and fantasies. "The theory of aggressive male domination over women as a natural right is so deeply embedded in our cultural value system," writes Susan Brownmiller, "that all recent attempts to expose it—in movies, television commercials or even in children's textbooks—have barely managed to scratch the surface." Mary Daly, the Catholic philosopher, complains bitterly but with justification that the so-called "sexual revolution" has in fact been "one more extension of the politics of rape, a New Morality of false liberation foisted upon women, who have been told to be free to be what women have always been, sex objects. The difference is simply that there is now social pressure for women to be available to any male at the beckon of a once-over, to be a nonprofessional whore."

Barbara Seaman expressed the fear that "a great many young women are merely swapping the old-fashioned sex-is-for-men sexual masochism of their mothers for a new type of self-punitive behavior. They are trying to copy the *worst* sexual behaviors of men—the promiscuity and exploitation. Sometimes they bed down with people who hardly attract them at all, merely to add another conquest to the 'list.' " Hite quoted this deeply-felt complaint in her volume on female sexuality: "If the Sexual Revolution implies the attitude that now women are 'free' too, and they can fuck strangers and fuck over the opposite sex, just the way men can, I think it's revolting. Women don't want to be 'free' to adopt the male model of sexuality; they want to be free to find their own." Another woman wrote: "It seems to me that the sexual revolution has just given the con men the chance to sell douches and razors, but that you don't see much in the way of real free expression and happiness, or joy in the body and in sex." As Hite pointed out, the effect of declaring sex healthy and women able and free to enjoy it has been to take away a woman's right to say no. Many, many women, she found, are fearful of asserting their own feelings because to do so would turn a partner off or damage his ego; and the result of keeping quiet is self-hatred, disgust, loneliness, and guilt.

Some women enjoy intercourse purely for physical pleasure or as an expression of interest in developing a relationship. Some are not ready for it unless they are confident of deep mutual love or commitment to a permanent relationship. Probably a majority, today, find it appropriate as a means of expressing closeness and intimacy with someone they like and trust. I'm not arguing for any particular preference, but only saying that women should assert their freedom to determine how they relate sexually to men. No woman, surely, should or need feel that she has to comply with some model of sexual behavior imposed by others. She should be free to determine her own preferences, to act in any way that expresses her own inner convictions or meets her personal needs. The psychoanalyst Leah Schaefer sums it up well: "The more thoughtful woman will realize that she must become her own authority in matters regarding her sexual conduct. She is obliged to create reasonable rules for herself. She must weight every edict, liberal or conservative, and discard those that do not make sense for her life. The only alternative is to succumb mindlessly to the latest fashions in sexuality—which may be as repressive as earlier, orthodox styles of sexual abstinence, and may introduce anxieties considerably more difficult to dismiss."

Oddly enough, the present dilemma in which you and so many other women find yourselves is in part due to the misreading, or misapplication of otherwise liberating knowledge. The discovery of the Pill and the availability of abortion, for example, have (as many nineteenth-century feminists anticipated) been interpreted to mean that because women can avoid or terminate pregnancy they will be ready to act sexually without any inhibitions. Men attribute their own sexual desires to women and assume, quite sincerely, that the only reason for their failure to jump into bed is the perpetuation of Victorian hangups. The muffled "not now" is taken as a mere concession to traditional but outmoded convention, and the male is more than ready to enlighten the modern female as to her "real" or "hidden" needs. It seldom occurs to the man that *even* if the woman is prepared for intercourse and equipped with safeguards, she may not find the attentions of this particular individual overwhelmingly attractive! According to one study, twenty-five percent of all women in this country feel that their first experience of intercourse involved an element of force or imposed pressure.

But an even more serious difficulty for women of your age is the influence of Masters and Johnson's study, *Human Sexual Response*, published in 1966. It provided scientific evidence for some important and liberating facts: women can enjoy orgasm more intensely and more frequently than males. But unfortunately some very unliberating conclusions have been drawn from these facts. It has become part of our sexual lore to assume that any woman of normal sexual capacity is capable of orgasmic response *as a result of coitus alone*—and that if she fails to do so she is either "frigid," or her partner is incompetent. *This deduction from Masters and Johnson is entirely invalid* and causes untold, unnecessary distress to women and to men. Let me explain why.

50:

In the first place, the Masters and Johnson sample of participants in their laboratory study was entirely unrepresentative of college women. Of their 382 female subjects, only two were under twenty-one, and 357 of these women were married or had been married. Thus most had had much more extensive sexual experience than any college student, and usually for an extended period with one male partner. But, secondly, we now know from later studies that the Masters and Johnson sample was unrepresentative of women as a whole. They were required as a condition of participation in the study to be regularly orgasmic during intercourse: later studies have shown that a majority of women need sensitive and extensive manual stimulation of the clitoral area if they are to have an orgasm. Only about a third regularly have an orgasm through stimulation by the penis. Most women in Hite's sample agreed that orgasm was important to them (though not all thought it essential to "good sex"), but many emphasized the importance of long-term, regular, sensitive partners if they were to receive the necessary manual stimulation to make orgasm possible, and others complained that the man tended to be uninterested in anything other than intercourse and his own climax. One objected strongly to the growing tendency to make orgasm a test of successful "performance": "The idea of having orgasms is important to me, but I can certainly enjoy sex without having them. Worse than not having an orgasm is the feeling that I've failed or that I'm frigid or unsexy. . . . I don't have sex to have an orgasm . . . but generally I have sex because I want to have a loving fucking tenderness with that person."

It is therefore clear that the chances that you or your peers will immediately enjoy orgasm during intercourse is small. By accepting the Masters and Johnson sample as a criterion for your expectations in intercourse, you set up an unrealistic ideal and virtually condemn yourself and your partner to being found wanting. When Germaine Greer lectured here a couple of years ago she asked women the question: "Why do you continue to engage in intercourse when you are the less likely to find it pleasurable and the more likely to suffer its consequences [in pregnancy]?" I suggest that you propose to Jim that there are ways by which both of you can have the satisfaction of orgasm and a sense of closeness *without* your doing more than you want or taking any risks. Of course, that does involve his compromising on his desire for intercourse; but doesn't he say he loves you a lot?

He may reply that his urge to have intercourse is due to biological or hormonal factors and that he cannot control it. He may be right in the premise, but he's surely wrong in the conclusion he draws. To what extent male/female differences are due to nature and to what extent to nurture is a complex matter about which the experts disagree. Anthropologists have established the fact that the roles of men and women can be greatly modified by learning, even if biological and hormonal factors establish some parameters that predispose each sex to certain types behavior. So there's no reason to suppose that men are incapable of learning sexual roles that take full account of their partner's preferences.

I think that the right way to defend your freedom is to claim that in a human society every person has the right to be an individual, to express her sexuality as she thinks appropriate, and to engage in whatever acts (including, of course, intercourse) she finds meaningful as a human being. And you can and must protest the apparatus of male-dominated culture that calls that right in question, however subtly. Women do not need to apologize for the fact that they are as sexual as men; equally, they do not need to apologize if they want to act sexually in a different way from men. If these differences are due to cultural factors they may disappear in time: the point is that you have a right to what you want *now*. If there are inborn distinctions these can contribute to the mutual fullness of sexual encounter rather than to oppression. Complementarity rather than identity, mutuality rather than duplication, openness to growth rather than static preservation of the past, freedom to be oneself rather than an anxious desire to conform, respect for each sex in its uniqueness rather than imposed similarity—these are surely what sexual freedom means.

I'm not sanguine that this view will prevail easily. You and your contemporaries will have to deal with deep-seated prejudices among men and widespread misperceptions among women. Hite found many men angry at being blamed for women's problems, threatened by women's abilities, and more concerned that women be supportive and docile than that they be autonomous. The *Playboy Report on American Men* showed that while "innovative" men like a lover to be intelligent, they are less enthusiastic about "someone who gets new and exciting ideas." Cultural forces that encourage girls in childhood and adolescence to see their value in terms of acceptance by males are still strong. On the other hand, the psychologist Sandra Bem recently found that a third of the subjects in a college sample showed androgynous traits—the capacity to break out of rigid gender-roles, to be comfortable both in initiating sex and responding to another person, and the flexibility to exhibit either masculine or feminine qualities depending on the situation.

seven:

MASTURBATION

To Paul

I'm not particularly surprised that your roommate is rather shocked at your uninhibited views about masturbation. Although almost all men masturbate at some time in their lives (though there's nothing wrong with those who don't), very few seem to be able to talk about it without embarrassment. Hite recently found that almost all her respondents made masturbation a regular part of their lives, whether they were single or married, but the overwhelming majority were secretive about the fact and most felt defensive or guilty—and this, remember, among a sample who can be presumed to be more liberal and open than the general population. There doesn't seen to be much sexual freedom here! Eighty percent of men under twenty-four responding to a *Playboy* questionnaire said they approved of the practice, yet I'm willing to bet you won't hear many of your friends volunteering the fact that they do it themselves. A student writing in a Berkeley paper once remarked: "Honest masturbation is better than a dishonest lay," but whereas you hear some guys boasting about their latest success in getting a woman into bed, you're not likely to hear anyone admitting that *instead* of scoring he was satisfied with jerking off because his date didn't want to be laid!

The fact that David has had a conservative religious upbringing probably had a good deal to do with his anxieties. Not only Catholics but many Protestants and orthodox Jews have been taught from infancy to regard masturbation with abhorrence. I devoted a good deal of my psychic energy in my teens fighting against what I then sincerely believed to be a practice condemned by God. This obsession goes back to the Jewish concern with the family and the perpetuation of the race (though prohibitions of masturbation are found in religious sources as early as 2700 B.C.). It was feared that if men wasted the seminal fluid, which was assumed to be limited in quantity, their capacity to father children would be reduced. The story of Onan in Genesis, chapter thirty-eight, was a dramatic lesson for young boys for centuries. I can vividly remember the impact of hearing the terrible fate meted out by God to the unfortunate man who "spilled his seed on the ground." Scholars of all faiths now recognize that the reason the early Hebrews thought God had slain Onan was not for masturbation but for failing in some way to fulfill a religious responsibility to his family (there's disagreement exactly how). But in later Judaism the "destruction of seed" came to be regarded as the gravest sin in the Torah, comparable to homicide because sperms were thought to be tiny living humans!

Christianity took over the Jewish tradition and added to the reasons for condemning masturbation a profound distaste for the "irrational" pleasure of orgasm (derived from the Stoics) and the theory that any use of the sexual organs except for reproductive purposes was unnatural (derived from Aristotle). The medieval church, which had what one scholar has called "a superstitious reverence for semen," regarded masturbation as a more serious sin than fornication, adultery, or even rape. My personal theory is that this was because it was the sexual temptation the monastic clergy found most threatening, and which they therefore thought the most horrible. Pope Paul VI as recently as 1975 condemned masturbation as "an intrinsically and seriously disordered act," and it is striking that even liberal Catholic thinkers, while no longer holding the view that every act of masturbation is seriously sinful, still cannot bring themselves to advise people to enjoy it. At best, they teach, it is a selfish pleasure that must be fought against. The guilt imposed on teenage boys until recently by all this was horrific. The novel *Portnoy's Complaint* effectively depicts the dilemma of a boy "perpetually in dread that his loathsomeness would be discovered" and yet "wholly incapable of keeping my paws from my dong once it started to climb up my belly." Some people, like David, continue to feel anxious into adulthood about a perfectly harmless form of sexual release.

That masturbation is in itself harmless no medical authority would deny today. But doctors have been at least as responsible for anxiety about the practice as theologians, in recent centuries. Ever since a physician named Tissot wrote *Onanism: A Treatise on the Disorders Produced by Masturbation* in the eighteenth century, respected medical men have attributed everything from paralysis, cancer, heart trouble, epilepsy, insanity and intellectual confusion to masturbation. Even in this century authorities such as Freud and Havelock Ellis were concerned about post-adolescent "autoeroticism" and feared it might lead to premature ejaculation or impotence. In the 1920s manufacturers of medical equipment were still advertising painful devices to be fitted on boys and girls to prevent them from "self-abuse." Until the 1940s the *Boy Scout's Handbook* warned about the weakness and disease resulting from the discharge of seminal fluid, and candidates for admission to the Naval Academy were rejected if they showed "evidences of masturbation" (whatever that meant!). Occasionally college students still suffer from fears of losing their hair, breaking out in acne, and going blind because they masturbate. And in 1971 Norman Mailer, in *The Prisoner of Sex*, declared that masturbation cripples people and ends in insanity! It would all be funny, if the effects of such nonsense on impressionable young men were not tragic.

The fact is that masturbation is a regular phase of early human development, part of the natural infantile exploration and enjoyment of the body—better described as "self-discovery" than as "self-abuse." Infant boys soon discover the pleasure of touching the penis, though ejaculation does not take place until puberty. Most psychiatrists recognize that masturbation serves not only to discharge sexual tension but to reduce anxiety, to express hostility in a nondestructive way, and to assert the individual's sexual identity. Far from being, as some have thought, a source of later sexual problems, masturbation is (according to Kinsey) a positive aid in preparing for satisfying experience in intercourse. It is never itself a cause of emotional illness, though it may be symptomatic of psychological problems if, for example, it becomes an escape from all sexual contacts or from social and academic responsibilities.

Some doctors and counselors still warn students against "excessive" masturbation and thereby merely substitute a new anxiety for the old one, since what is excessive is never defined. Physical harm from masturbation is, in fact, impossible. The capacity for further arousal is exhausted long before any harm can be done to the system. Frequent ejaculation does not affect the male's capacity for later sexual activity or his fertility, since sperms and semen are continually produced by the testicles, seminal vesicles and prostate. There is no evidence to support the widely held myth that masturbation adversely affects academic or athletic performance. It may, on the contrary, help by reducing unnecessary tension. It is surely better to masturbate and sleep soundly than to spend a restless night fighting off a need for sexual release.

If masturbation were accepted as the normal phenomenon it is, no more reprehensible than wet dreams for a boy or menstruation for a girl, a great deal of anxiety and suffering would be avoided. To condemn it as wicked or sinful is as stupid as to punish a baby for crying when it is hungry or a child for wanting to climb trees. It only has undesirable consequences when it is associated with guilt and fear based on ignorance or an irrational, dogmatic denial of physical pleasure. Indeed masturbation has a number of very positive uses beyond adolescence. If every time a male felt the need for sexual release he had to find and use a female body there would be a lot more coercive and destructive sexual activity. Some men find that the problem of premature ejaculation can be helped if they masturbate before engaging in intercourse. At times when interpersonal sexual relations are impossible or interrupted by sickness, pregnancy or separation, men of all ages commonly find satisfaction in masturbation.

Why, then, are so many people embarrassed about masturbation long after they have learned to be open and uninhibited about other sexual matters? Obviously, in our culture, the heavy religious condemnation of the practice continues to have a direct effect, as it does on David. In those cultures that encourage early genital play there is no such guilt. But I think other explanations must be sought for the widespread sense of embarrassment about masturbation even in non-religious people. As infants most boys have been strongly discouraged from handling their genitals, except for urination, and they internalize these prohibitions. Masturbation in early childhood is enjoyable but also threatening because of this parental condemnation—and mysterious because every other pleasurable experience of infancy is encouraged. These deeply-rooted doubts are given new intensity at puberty when ejaculation occurs. The sense of parental disapproval is underscored when a boy's mother maintains an uncharacteristic silence over soiled sheets after nocturnal emissions or masturbation: apparently, this is something so despicable that it cannot even be discussed! When a boy first ejaculates he may be shocked at the intensity of the pleasure involved or afraid that he has damaged himself. Since they are usually totally unprepared by adults, boys often report terror because they think they are bleeding, discharging pus, or internally injured. "I thought that whatever had felt like it was breaking, had broken. I'd ruined it for ever. I was scared and felt guilty and sinful. Plus I had to clean it up or my mother would find out. I swore to all the powers that be, if only it would be all right, and no one would find out, I'd never do it again." This comment recalls the old myth, going back at least to Tissot and expressed by General Ripper in *Dr. Strangelove*, that semen is an essential "body fluid."

But there is a psychological dimension to a boy's masturbation at puberty—it represents the first real separation from his parents, the expression of his independent sexual identity. It has been said that you have to fall out of love with your mother before you can fall in love with a girl. In a way adolescent masturbation is the first step in this profound, usually unconscious breaking away from infantile sexual dependence. Not only has a prohibition imposed by parents been violated; the result has been found to be wonderfully pleasurable and the wisdom of the adult world is called in question. The myth of Adam and Eve has been played out again and the threats of the Father have been found to be false: disobedience has brought unimagined new vistas of happiness rather than disaster. But it has also brought guilt, and loss of innocence and separation. And I suspect that we never quite get over that traumatic event.

It may be that there is an element of dissatisfaction built into masturbatory orgasm. Both men and women report that while they find the intensity of pleasure in masturbation greater, they find the personal and physical closeness of intercourse more satisfying. Masturbation is, after all, a solitary activity (though *not* the "solitary vice") and solitary sex is almost by definition deficient. I've emphasized that masturbation can be an entirely mature and valuable form of sexual release throughout life, but that is not to say that it is totally fulfilling or ideal. I think we make a mistake if we swing from embarrassment over masturbation to elevating it as the acme of sexual satisfaction—like Dr. Krankheit in *Candy* who recommended it as "the only sex-mode that permits complete fulfillment and mental health." Sex is interpersonal and masturbation is at best a prelude or an interlude. It may be more natural or moral than interpersonal activity that is deceitful, phony or exploitative, but it cannot satisfy the whole being in the way that truly mutual interaction does. Thus perhaps a certain degree of dissatisfaction or frustration, perpetuating the anxiety and guilt associated with adolescent experience, is unavoidable. It has been suggested that the guilt associated with the incest taboo may serve the useful purpose of encouraging the child to find appropriate sexual partners outside the family: in the same way, the sense of failure and imperfection associated with masturbation may encourage us to pursue the fuller realization of mature sexuality with another person.

Morton Hunt in his study of sexual behavior undertaken for *Playboy* made this helpful comment: "It is not truly liberated, for example, to use masturbation as a continuing substitute for heterosexual relationships that are available but anxiety producing. In the great majority of adolescents and teenagers, masturbation is developmental—it is a normal part of the maturation process and serves as a valuable precursor of heterosexual intercourse for which the immature are not psychologically or socially ready, but toward which they move, step by step. . . . Some young people who are particularly troubled by feelings of personal inadequacy and inferiority find it exceedingly difficult to take those steps to establish relationships with the opposite sex, and for them masturbation may be supportive as a crutch is, weakening rather than strengthening them. The case is similar with adults who lose a mate through divorce or death. Most of them use masturbation as a helpful substitute until they establish new relationships, but a minority, lacking self-confidence or ego strength, may come to rely on it and use it as a way to avoid making the effort to seek another partner."

Remember that David has a right to his religious difficulties with masturbation, and don't add your condemnation to the guilt he already has. He must work his own way to freedom, and even the most rational arguments can't wipe away years of indoctrination. But people do change their attitudes—even deeply entrenched ones. I know: my own views have come round about 180 degrees since I was your age!

eight:
SELF-PLEASURING

To Jane

After I'd written my last letter on sexual freedom for women I came across Lonnie Garfield Barbach's book *For Yourself* and it helped to bring into focus for me another aspect of female liberation that I think you should be aware of. Barbach and many others are arguing that if women are to be able to assert their own independence and to insist on their rights when it comes to deciding what forms of sexual intimacy are enjoyed, they need first of all to learn to achieve their own sexual arousal, including orgasm, *without* male involvement. The search for the "liberated orgasm" has too often meant the search for the "magic penis" that will alone make possible a woman's satisfaction. One widely read book, *The Sensuous Woman* by "J," urged women to develop their capacities for sexual enjoyment, but only on the assumption that "we were designed to delight, excite and satisfy the male of the species"—thus once again reducing women to the status of appendages to male interests. Women are still encouraged to take their cues about sex from men and to accommodate their sexual fantasies and expectations to a male-centered version of the world. What is needed, many women feel, is a direct challenge to this cultural tradition that makes intercourse *the* form of sexual satisfaction.

Masturbation is the obvious candidate for attention if this goal is adopted, for not only is it something that a woman can engage in by herself, it is also by far the most reliable means by which women attain orgasm. There is a lot to be said, therefore, for women learning not only to have orgasms by masturbation but, even more importantly, to enjoy them without guilt and to integrate the practice into their sexual lives as a positive growth experience. "Masturbation is sex on a solo level—that's like saying I can take care of myself. Get in touch with my body and self. I am *here*. I am sexy. I am okay. I like myself." "Masturbation is important for women who are taught to rely on men for sexual satisfaction and who are taught our bodies are ugly and mysterious. And that's just about *all* of us." These two statements from Hite's book seem to me entirely sound, provided two qualifications are kept in mind. First, recognize that our cultural value system has laid a heavy burden of guilt on masturbation, especially for those with a strict religious upbringing. While it is entirely appropriate to try to help such women to rid themselves of this inhibition, it is easier for them to give intellectual assent to your arguments than it is to escape the internal self-condemnation with which they have been indoctrinated. You must be sensitive in such cases. It is obviously as undesirable for a woman to feel she *must* masturbate to conform to the new model of liberation as it is for her to feel she must *not* masturbate to conform to the old religious taboos. Don't add to the guilt such a woman already bears the additional burden of feeling inadequate because she cannot easily undo years of childhood miseducation. Many women who have never masturbated still develop completely adequate relationships.

Secondly, it is a main concern of mine to help you get away from the idea that orgasm is the be-all and end-all of sexuality. So while it may be important, in order to redress the imbalance caused by our traditional indifference to female sexual pleasure, to focus attention on masturbatory orgasm, don't allow this to exclude other forms of self-pleasuring. Your goal should be to learn to appreciate and enjoy the erogenous capacities of the whole body (not only of those well known "zones"). You need to learn pride and pleasure in your distinctive body shape, color and texture whether or not it conforms to the current male ideal represented by the playmate of the month. An obsessive concern with being slim is something men have imposed on you and one consequence (tragically manifested in anorexia and bulimarexia) is a repudiation of one's body.

If women are to be in a position to enter into sexual and loving relationships as equals they have to learn basic self-esteem. The woman who has no security about her worth as a person and a sexual being cannot share confidently in love with a partner. An English author put it well some years ago (I've modified his use of the masculine pronouns): "She who is able to love herself is able to love others also, for she has understood her true value and does not need to bolster up her own value by snatching it from others. When I am unaware of what I truly am, I am incapable of giving myself value, and so I desperately seek value from someone else; and this leads me to action which is sometimes identified with sex; but with sex divorced from its true object, which is the completion of the union of two people who have found their own value, and therefore found value in each other."

Learning the art of self-pleasuring through masturbation and whole-body sensitivity not only gives women a new confidence in their own bodies but a new understanding of their personal sexuality. It can be a form of therapy that reduces the likelihood of unresponsiveness in later interpersonal relationships. Because orgasmic women are, as recent research suggests, more self-confident, insightful and understanding, they are better equipped to respond to others and to share their own richness. "Masturbation teaches you to know your own body, and to gratify it, which leads to increasing your sense of independence and may also increase your ability to relate to someone else; being able to tell someone else what gives one pleasure can do a lot for a relationship." Sexual satisfaction is a more individual and complicated affair for a woman than it is for a man, and if you are to help a partner satisfy your needs it can be important to know how to do so yourself. Some authorities feel that a history of effective masturbation is almost essential if sexual interaction between two people is to be fully enjoyed. The fear that some women have, of being too dependent on a man if they abandon themselves to orgasm with him, can be overcome if that experience has first been discovered for oneself. Women who are skilled at pleasuring themselves will be better able to stimulate their partners —something that many men want and feel deprived of.

There will, of course, be men who resist the idea that women should learn to satisfy themselves—since this implies that the male role is less vital than we like to imagine. Some men indeed still refuse to believe that female orgasm is *possible* without a male contribution. The fact is that our culture has persistently down-played the significance of female sexual pleasure, except in so far as it is a byproduct of intercourse. This indifference has been due to several factors. Women have simply not been considered important and their enjoyment of sex, even when its existence has been acknowledged, has been thought accidental. Female orgasm is not essential to reproduction, as the male's is, and reproduction has been the name of the game. Thus even though religious authorities have condemned female masturbation as well as male, the penalties for it and the attention given to it have been far less, since it does not involve the loss of that precious life-giving fluid. Finally, for centuries sheer ignorance of female biology and of the role of the clitoris contributed to the silence. The *Oxford English Dictionary* records only two uses of the word clitoris (in medical texts) before the nineteenth century. And when the existence of the organ was publicly acknowledged, clitoridectomy, intended to relieve female patients of hysteria, epilepsy, and convulsions, was practiced, particularly in Britain and the United States, until well into this century. It is difficult to avoid the conclusion that unconscious fears of a threat to male sexual dominance underlay this medical persecution of women.

The elimination of the clitoris and the denial of woman's sexuality as an independent, healthy phenomenon was effected with greater subtlety by Sigmund Freud. Freud, who admitted that feminine sexuality was "an impenetrable obscurity," nevertheless turned his brilliant mind to the subject with disastrous results! He concluded that the psychological problems of many women were due to a failure to transfer erotic focus from the clitoral orgasm appropriate to childhood to the vaginal orgasm appropriate to adulthood. "With the change to femininity," wrote Freud, "the clitoris should wholly or in part hand over its sensitivity and, at the same time, its importance to the vagina." The basic assumption was that feminine maturity is necessarily associated with intercourse and the vagina; the incidental implication was that a woman's sexual potential can only be realized with the help of a penis. It was therefore obvious that masturbatory self-arousal was immature and liable to interfere with "normal" sexual satisfaction in adulthood. For decades women who masturbated and/or failed to have "vaginal orgasms" were taught that they were inadequate or even perverse. The idea is not dead: in a 1975 series of essays by psychoanalysts I came across this statement: "The adolescent girl . . . must not masturbate so much that her sexual gratification is fixed on her own body, and fantasies of being able to satisfy herself are promoted at the expense of accepting the need for vaginal penetration in coitus."

This misleading Freudian myth has undergone a series of critical assaults. First Kinsey, in 1953, found that clitoral masturbation to orgasm, far from endangering the achievement of orgasm during intercourse, actually made that three times more likely. Masters and Johnson, in 1966, established that the physiological process of orgasm, whether produced by masturbation, petting or intercourse, is identical. Mary Jane Sherfey, in 1972, showed that when orgasm takes place during intercourse it is the friction of the labia minora on the clitoral hood, caused indirectly by the thrusting of the penis, that is responsible. While a coital orgasm may be felt by the woman to be centered in the vagina, which contracts rhythmically, that organ actually has relatively few nerve-endings and the real focus of intense pleasure is in the clitoris. The clitoris is in some respects homologous to the penis (Sherfey has suggested that we should call the penis an "exaggerated clitoris" rather than vice versa); but its stimulation, either in masturbation or in intercourse, has to be indirect—so that to come to orgasm in masturbation is biologically the same experience as to do so in coitus.

The final blow to the Freudian theory, of course, was the recognition, mentioned in my last letter, that only a minority of women regularly experience coital orgasm. If Freud were right we would have to conclude that a large majority of women never achieve sexual maturity—that seventy percent or more are dysfunctional: a ridiculous proposition. It is now generally accepted, therefore, that for a woman to enjoy orgasm through masturbation or manual stimulation by a partner is entirely normal and healthy.

It would be a mistake, however, to go to the other extreme and suppose that intercourse is unimportant for women when they are ready for it. Those who experience orgasm both in masturbation and in intercourse frequently say they find the former more intense but the latter more psychologically satisfying because of the whole-body closeness it involves when a relationship is truly mutual. There is something inevitably lonely and incomplete about masturbation. "It was really boring because I was by myself and there was nobody there," said one woman during a discussion. The solution, for those who do not reach orgasm during intercourse itself, is to enjoy the closeness of intimacy with a partner in intercourse, and orgasmic satisfaction through manual stimulation of the clitoral area before, during or after intercourse. There is no reason to doubt that self-pleasuring in masturbation can be a valuable (and for some a necessary) preparation for sexual fulfillment.

Reaching this rational or empirical conclusion will not,

alas, free women from the hangups over masturbation under which so many labor even now. Parental and cultural pressures, even among your liberated peers, have usually established deeply entrenched psychological blocks that cannot be easily dissolved. The trouble begins in early infancy. Baby girls enjoy stroking their genitals from the first years of life and apparent orgasm has been observed as early as four-months-old. But, unfortunately, parental reaction to erotic behavior is usually repressive—probably a reflection of their uneasiness with their own sexuality, which even a small child can sense. The idea that self-pleasuring is unnatural is communicated in subtle ways, if not by direct prohibition. Enjoyment of every other part of the body, and of other forms of exploration are encouraged and celebrated: genital play is frowned on and attempts are made at least to distract the infant's attention. Whereas little boys are applauded when they handle their penis to urinate, small girls are usually given no encouragement to discover how their genitals function or how the urethra is separate from the anus (let alone the vagina, the very existence of which is frequently unknown to pre-pubertal girls). The result is profound confusion and a widespread tendency to associate the whole genital area with the "dirty" anus and the act of defecation. One observer has noted that a mother showed a little boy his body in a mirror some months earlier than she showed her baby girl. From an early age, tiny girls are encouraged to wear swimsuits that cover their (not-yet-existent) breasts, while boys have much greater freedom to display and see their bodies. It is not surprising that so many women suffer from a sense that their bodies are ugly, misshapen, unattractive and undesirable.

It is well known that the number of girls who masturbate during adolescence is significantly lower than the number of boys—though the number of women who masturbate at some time in their lives is now as high as seventy-five percent. One reason is probably the lower level of genital awareness due to the interior nature of the female organs compared to the penis and testicles; boys have erections from birth (and possibly before). "The boy's sexual development is comparatively simple and linear" says the psychologist Judith Bardwick. "The extremely erotic penis, which has been perceptually dominant since earliest childhood, remains the executor of his sexuality. The girl is less invested in the genitals and genital sexuality because of the internal nature of her reproductive organs and the lesser sensitivity of those organs."

A second factor inhibiting adolescent female sexual experimentation, in addition to religious and parental prohibitions (that may be even stronger than they are for boys), is the lack of a network of peer pressures and information which, among their brothers, leaves very few unaware of the exciting new possibilities of adolescence. Again, adolescent boys are given subtle messages by adults, whatever the official ideals may be, to the effect that it is time they began to demonstrate their masculinity through sexual activity of various kinds. Adolescent girls are warned of the *dangers* of allowing themselves to be carried away by sexual desire, lest their official role as the referee in dating be compromised. Sex education does not usually mention the role of pleasure in sex, except in terms of warning: one friend of mine was brought up in a convent where she was forbidden to wear shiny shoes lest she see her undergarments reflected and be led into temptation! All of this discourages masturbation and adds to the guilt and fear when orgasm is experienced.

A further problem distinctive to women arises because menstruation begins about the same time as pubertal sexual arousal. The initial experience is at best messy, frequently emotionally demanding and sometimes painful. However much menstruation may have positive implications for future motherhood, it seems to me its beginning (often quite unprepared for) must frequently lead to negative feelings about the awakening of sexual interests. Lorna and Philip Sarrel point out that anxiety can also be increased by the discharge experienced by most girls before they begin menstruating, by problems with the insertion or removal of tampons, or by a painful or embarrassing first pelvic exam. Combined with lingering cultural taboos about menstrual blood, these can all contribute to a sense of awkwardness and embarrassment about the physical changes of adolescence and about sexuality. Only a steady improvement in social attitudes and a determined effort by women and by liberated men to confront these subtle distortions will overcome an entirely unfair and unnecessary barrier to sexual freedom. One student wrote in the log of our women's center that she believed a woman was not free until she had tasted her menstrual blood: maybe some profound symbolic act is needed to exorcise the demons of superstition and oppression.

Lonnie Barbach reports great success with helping women through small-group therapy, and you may have friends who need this kind of support. But her book includes instructions for a series of exercises that a woman can undertake on her own, and those students to whom I've lent *For Yourself* tell me they've found it extremely valuable.

nine:
MUTUALITY

To Paul and Jane

I'm sending this letter to both of you because it represents the core—I might even say the climax!—of what I've been writing over the past weeks. I've argued that sexual freedom means liberation from false myths, from the subtle antagonisms inherent in conventional dating, and from the traditional roles of dominant masculinity and submissive femininity. I've urged you to be free to develop a personal sexual identity consistent with humane values that you have established for yourselves. But there's clearly a potential snag in all this: however satisfying masturbation may be, sex is essentially an interpersonal experience, and as you develop your own pattern of meaningful sexual activity you inevitably run into conflict, or at least tension, with the desires and standards of a partner.

There's no way to avoid situations that are painful and even anguishing as you experiment with sex. But I do believe that much confusion and suffering can be avoided if sexual relationships are integrated with the whole self, and if you learn to relate to others with warmth and openness. Mutuality, I suggest, should be the goal rather than the achievement or granting of sexual favors. The typical maneuvering for position, the need for deceptive covering, and hesitation about verbalizing one's real preferences are all inconsistent with sexual freedom. Sexuality can be a matter of joyous exploration, not of anxious grappling for advantage. Men and women can learn to relax in the pleasure of growing personal and physical intimacy without feeling pressure to rush to orgasmic discharge. Kissing, fondling, caressing and petting can be enjoyed for their own value as satisfying means of interpersonal union, instead of being checked off on a list of foothills to be scaled as quickly as possible before conquering Mount Climax.

So long as either partner feels it necessary to put on a front, or fears that more will be expected than he or she is ready to give, the basic trust that is essential to any deep human relationship is undercut. Each participant in truly mutual sexuality has to be ready to put into words the real meaning of those silent signals and to be ready to respond to the hesitations, hopes, fears and joys of the *other*. The man must be prepared to admit his need of help in developing sensitivity and to be satisfied and happy with alternative forms of closeness when the relationship does not require or cannot sustain intercourse. The woman must be liberated to express her sexual needs, whether they be more or less genital than the man's, and to value herself as an independent being. Both partners must be set free from the obsession with sex as a performance, in which the skill or response of the participants is measured as success or failure. As long as sex is used to demonstrate prowess, or even sensitivity, and as long as one is worried about being found inadequate in physical response, there is no real openness of the self to another, no freedom to trust, no truly mutual sex.

Such an understanding of sexuality puts the question of intercourse in a new context. Different types of intimacy will be found appropriate for different degrees of communication and closeness with a partner. There may be a steady progression from kissing to necking, from necking to petting, from petting to oral sex, from oral sex to intercourse—or the order may be quite different. In any case, each stage will be a natural, mutually accepted reflection of a growing understanding. In some cases the later stages will never be reached, either because the relationship is terminated or because it proves to have lmited physical significance. Indeed, to speak of "stages" as if they represented clearly defined way stations on a journey towards a specific destination, which alone gives them meaning, becomes inappropriate. The sensitivity and responsiveness of the whole body is appreciated for its own worth and given its proper valuation in the context of the relationship. Thus some people will continue for months, perhaps for life, to enjoy kissing, fondling and hugging each other without any sense of pressure to engage in genital contact. Some, who want to preserve the special intimacy of intercourse for a permanent commitment, will find other ways of sharing the pleasures of orgasm with a lover.

Because what I have just said is likely to be misunderstood as an exhortation to avoid intercourse, let me hasten to emphasize that this is not my intention. In my view *both* the traditional ideal of premarital chastity *and* the modern assumption that intercourse is inevitable and essential in a sexual relationship involve an unfortunate isolation of one sex act from the wider range of sexually satisfying experiences. There is surely something absurd about the fact that we can say, in all seriousness, of a couple who are deeply in love and planning marriage, but not sleeping together, that "They are not having sex." Sex isn't something we *do*, it's something we *have* from birth and all of us have sex before we're married! I don't advocate "the new celibacy" that celebrates what *Newsweek* called "the joy of not having sex," and I think that attempts to put the genie of the sexual revolution back in the bottle and persuade teenagers to rejoin the Victorian age are doomed to failure. I do believe that so long as intercourse is treated as an end in itself (whether one to be sought or denied), people will often be hurt, used, deceived, disappointed and stunted in their growth to sexual maturity. Whether a particular relationship includes intercourse seems to me a secondary issue: what matters is whether the individuals concerned are growing in their capacity for closeness, self-giving and caring.

Anthony Storr put this so well that I repeat his words with some minor modifications: "Sexual intercourse may be said to be one aspect, perhaps the most basic and most important aspect, of a relationship between persons. In ideally mature form, it is a relationship between a man and a woman in which giving and taking is equal, and in which the genitals are the most important channel through which love is expressed and received. It is one of the most natural, most rewarding and most life-enhancing, of all human experiences. . . . But this wonderfully enriching experience is only possible when the two people concerned have achieved a relationship in which, during the actual process of lovemaking, each is able to confront the other exactly as they are, with no reserves and no pretenses, and in which there is no admixture of childish dependence or fear."

Unfortunately the identification of sex and sexual intercourse is still far from uncommon, and many people are dedicated to the pursuit of "organ grinding." All too often it is "scoring," "getting laid," "balling" that counts: all other activities are incidental or mere foreplay. "Sex, like work, becomes a matter of performance. There is always a goal in view—ejaculation for the man, orgasm for the woman. . . . Sex, for them, is not a way of being, a way of expressing identity or feelings, or a way of nourishing a commitment. It is always a single incident, an occasion, an accomplishment." Those words were written by Masters and Johnson, who are frequently thought to have encouraged the current obsession with orgasm. They go on to say that "usually, goal-oriented sex is self-defeating." Shere Hite found that among the men in her survey the traditional sequence of foreplay, intercourse and male orgasm was still taken for granted. When asked, "What is the place of intercourse in sex? Would you like to change the definition of sex so that it was not so rigidly focused on erection and intercourse?" the largest percentage of her respondents *simply couldn't understand the question*, and most felt that male orgasm is the point of sex and intercourse. Hite concluded that even those who were interested in exploring other forms of sexual stimulation felt great cultural pressures to "perform" in intercourse.

Ultimately the great majority of women and men want the same three things in sex: 1) intercourse, 2) orgasm, and

3) closeness with another human being. The difficulty arises because they differ in their priorities and in their assumptions about the relation between the three. Men seek intercourse first because of cultural expectations and perhaps because of biological instinct; they *usually* get orgasm, however unreceptive the women may be; they hope they will find closeness but they are sometimes disappointed and (to judge from the comments of women) even more frequently kid themselves into thinking a closeness exists where none does. Many of Hite's male samples, when asked "why do you *like* intercourse?" gave "physical closeness, overall body contact, and the feeling of being loved and accepted" as primary concerns. But many, because of their ignorance of female biology and psychology do not receive the response they hope for. Most women feel that men still approach sex with little real interest in their pleasure: "I feel during foreplay like I'm being condescended to, dealt with, like he's going through a necessary inconvenience." The problem may be more one of understanding than of good will. A recent survey of psychiatrists found that they thought three out of four men *attempt* to satisfy their partners, though less than half are actually sensitive to a woman's needs. Another Hite respondent wrote: "There have been several men who seemed to care whether I was happy, but they wanted to make me feel happy according to *their* conception of what ought to do it (fucking harder or longer or whatever) and acted as if it was damned impertinent of me to suggest that my responses weren't programmed exactly like those of mythical women in the classics of porn."

Women seem to put greater emphasis on the search for closeness and frequently engage in intercourse in the hope that this will result. Women replying to the question put by Judith Bardwick, "Why do you make love?" typically replied "because it's a means of getting closer to him" and "it's a way of reaching people." But if the relationship is not one of mutuality and sensitivity this hope is usually ill-founded and the woman finishes up without closeness *or* orgasm, since the foreplay involved is seldom satisfying. Women replying to Hite complained that most men—particularly those in relatively new relationships—lacked the knowledge or interest to respond to their desires: "Men have been brainwashed to think they're the sexual experts, and furthermore, that whatever feels good to them is what feels good and 'fulfills' us also. Most men I have slept with seemed to have the attitude, 'Here, dear, let me show you how.' Of all the presumption." A woman wrote in the log of our women's center: "Sex is filthy and painful when you do it for the wrong reasons and with the wrong person. . . . How many men in college really know how to treat a woman in bed? Not many, because they are young and still learning. They have this 'I came to conquer' attitude toward the whole act and do not take time to enjoy and revel in the experience."

The ideal would be, perhaps, if we could learn to experience intercourse, orgasm and closeness simultaneously, but that is an unrealistic goal. Indeed, there are those who argue that sequential orgasm is preferable, in principle, since concern with the needs of one's partner, even in the most mature relationship, is liable to interfere with or inhibit one's own orgasmic abandon. The best that college students can hope to achieve is that each partner eventually enjoys each of the desired goals in whatever order is acceptable. But that requires a realistic recognition that intercourse may have to be postponed in the interests of mutuality until both partners are fully prepared for it. This does, frequently, involve some restraint—usually on the part of the male. But it has several profound advantages: he is much more likely to find the ultimate act of intimacy, when it is attempted, truly an experience of union, she is much more likely to be orgasmic during petting, both will enjoy precoital pleasures that are otherwise bypassed, and the effective use of contraception will be made much more likely.

I want to be more specific about what this means in practice, so I'll pursue the subject in my next letter.

ten:
COMMUNICATION

To Jane and Paul

There is one essential key to the freedom of sexual mutuality: *communication*. Nothing I can tell you and nothing you can pick up in the most complete do-it-yourself guide to sex is going to solve the problem of frustration or embarrassment or dissatisfaction between two people unless they succeed in communicating effectively with each other. Both men and women vary greatly in their individual sexual responses, and satisfaction of these needs with the consequent sense of closeness and merging together is not going to come about by mere chemistry or just because you are deeply in love. As it is, a conspiracy of silence often leads to increasingly complicated misunderstandings. If a woman enjoys a man's company she may accept intimacies she's unenthusiastic about because of his importunity and then resent his going ahead, even though she has kept quiet. She may assume that because *for her* passionate lovemaking would represent a serious commitment, it must be so for a male. He, for his part, may assume that for her, as for him, heavy petting is a natural preliminary to intercourse. Or he may think that because she appears to enjoy intercourse, it involved orgasmic satisfaction for her as surely as it did for him.

Partly because you live in a transition period, the interpretation of nonverbal signals is especially difficult. There was a time, not so long ago, when the established indicators of sexual availability or arousal (often varying in detail from community to community) were reasonably adequate guides to a person's readiness for further action. Nowadays the scene is more complicated. Without intending to be "cock-teasers" women assume the right to dress as casually and freely as men—but it's difficult for males not to interpret their signals quite wrongly. Men tend to assume that a woman without a bra is by definition "an easy ball" or "a sure thing," when all she may be interested in is comfort. Tight jeans are frequently assumed to be a "come-on." Indeed, according to some researchers in Los Angeles, males tend to read the signals they want to see in such innocuous things as the place where a woman agrees to meet them or purely conventional compliments on their looks or athletic build. The sociologist Jessie Bernard put the point very nicely: "Most men refuse to believe, or cannot believe, that the nubile young woman, luscious in her tennis shorts or bikini, is not deliberately signaling a come-on. But the signal is not necessarily the one the men pick up. She may be asking for admiration: the man hopes she is asking for him. Her body keeps signaling: I am a desirable woman. The men who see her reply, Don't be so damn provocative about it unless you want us to make something of it. The clothes, designed by knowing men, seem to signal clear and loud, Take me! The girl may actually mean nothing more than, Admire me."

The same ambiguity in communication carries over into sexual intimacy with equally unfortunate results. A woman feels embarrassed about telling a partner if he is failing to give her the kind of stimulation she needs: "Yes, sometimes I feel guilty, or like I'm intruding, bothering him. I *know* it's ridiculous and masochistic, but I still *do*." Although men told Hite that they enjoyed and wanted other forms of sexual play, they often felt it incumbent on them to act out the part of the male performer and then blamed women for not taking the initiative. Lonnie Barbach, in her new book, *Shared Intimacies*, points out something that is obvious when you consider it: the absurdity of supposing that because someone loves you, she or he is able to read your mind! Barbach suggests that the problem arises for women in part because they have not until recently been accustomed to talk about sex together, and thus have no language available to deal with the subject. But she also recognizes that there is a fundamental insecurity in male sexual behavior—men feel they have to succeed and have to maintain an erection to do so—that has made women hesitant to make suggestions, lest this be interpreted as criticism. A solution for many women is to reinforce specific behavior they do find enjoyable by verbally indicating their pleasure to their partner. And although many of Barbach's clients were initially inclined to accept considerable discomfort and dissatisfaction for themselves, rather than risk upsetting their lovers, none of them received a negative response once they took the step and opened up a conversation.

The first thing a couple needs to discover is the satisfaction to be had from kissing and touching the body. In the rush to orgasm your generation often denies itself pleasures that in my day were enjoyed for months: indeed I feel fortunate that your mother and I have been able, throughout our marriage, to discover over several years many of the joys of sex that are often stale for today's students before they leave college. Hite found that quite a few older women had stronger sexual feeling during "necking" or "making out," before sex always implied intercourse, and she quotes this nostalgic memory of one man's earliest sex experience: "When I was seventeen and still a virgin, I was more in love than I have ever been, before or since. The girl was also a virgin. We went on a picnic in the mountains and were together alone all day. Though we didn't have intercourse or even heavy petting, we were both highly satisfied emotionally. I think that that first experience in love has colored all my relationships with women I have known since then and has made me more interested in long foreplay, tenderness, and seeking the ultimate pleasure of my sex partner."

As Mary Calderone and Eric Johnson have recently

stressed, all of the skin is potentially erotic and "a most important part of the sexual system." An exaggerated emphasis on the "erogenous zones" has discouraged people from exploring the potential joys of full-body massage or kissing. Both men and women vary in the sensitivity of different parts of the body: for example, some women are hardly aroused by touching the breasts (particularly near menstruation) and some men discover that their nipples are highly sensitive. While one partner explores the other's body she or he needs to be told which motions or touches are most pleasurable.

Many college students discover that it is not necessary to insert a penis into a vagina in order to have a gratifying relationship and that full-body contact can be adequately enjoyed by sleeping together without intercourse. A survey on one campus found that two out of three responding students had slept with a member of the other sex all night without engaging in coitus. Of course, if ejaculation takes place close to the vagina it is wise to use some form of contraceptive just in case—but the fact that a woman is prepared for this eventuality should not be taken as a silent signal that she is necessarily ready for intercourse.

Probably the most widely practiced alternative to intercourse is mutual masturbation or petting to orgasm (Masters and Johnson call it "partner manipulation"). If sensitively undertaken it provides a deep sense of mutual physical and psychological intimacy without the risk of pregnancy or the problems some women have with intercourse. But this too needs to be practiced and learned: neither partner knows instinctively what is effective for the other and it's stupid to progress to other activities simply because the first fumbling attempt is less than ecstatically successful. Women do not immediately understand how to handle the male penis and testicles in order to give maximum satisfaction, any more than men know instinctively how to stimulate the clitoris. But the experience can be of great importance as an indication of love and warmth: "It feels nice when my partner strokes my penis. I like it a lot. It gives a cozy feeling, a feeling of total acceptance and comfortability. I'm ready to give myself more to her then." Stimulation of a woman to orgasm is even more difficult for a man to learn and often depends on her ability, either by words or by guiding the man's hands, to communicate her individual preferences. Some therapists believe that it may sometimes be necessary for a couple to watch each other masturbate by themselves in order to understand what differentiates them. Many men suppose that a woman is best aroused by the insertion of a finger or fingers in the vagina; although that is helpful to some, the vagina is not for most a primary source of pleasure. Very gentle massage of the inner lips and of the shaft of the clitoris is often effective, but in some cases or at some point deeper pressure may be needed: again, sensitivity to each person's needs is vital. Although some men initially feel embarrassed or incompetent to help a partner achieve orgasm, many find great satisfaction and erotic pleasure when they succeed in doing so. "It is beautiful to see a woman having orgasm out of your stimulation, your direct stimulation without being worried with your sexual performance. It is also very arousing, and together with the caressing that's possible (most people have two hands . . . and a mouth), it becomes a great experience."

Oral sex is a practice that in my day came later in sexual activity, but people of your generation seem to accept it as a preliminary or alternative to intercourse. Morton Hunt's survey found that two out of three college-age men and women had experienced some oral sex. It doesn't carry the dangers of pregnancy (though it can be the means of transmitting venereal disease) and it represents for many a valuable expression of affection and mutuality: "I enjoy cunnilingus immensely for the obvious physical reason, and for a mental reason as well. The male is exhibiting positive feelings to my femaleness. . . . For him to declare by action that the penis isn't necessary for my orgasm is to offer himself as a human being first and a male second." What is essential, if oral sex is to unify rather to divide, is that both partners feel entirely comfortable with the activity. Some men have profound cultural inhibitions about cunnilingus, others find the taste and odor of the female genitals unappealing and some women are uneasy with it for the same reason. Many women have difficulty performing fellatio: the penis is not a beautiful organ to most people and semen, though totally harmless, is not exactly tasty. A few people may have anxieties about the (largely pro forma) fact that the practice is illegal in many places. However sexist, mistaken or irrational such hesitations may seem, to pressure a partner into oral sex unwillingly is inconsistent with treating him or her as a person. One woman, pressured to perform fellatio, said she felt as if her face was being raped. In the context of mutual growth in intimacy such inhibitions may eventually disappear, but their reality cannot be denied or eliminated by a brief lesson in biology or sexual techniques.

I must admit that anal intercourse doesn't appeal to me at all, though like most people I'm aware of the erotic sensitivity of the rectal area. But it's a practice that has a long history of use as a method of birth control and during menstruation. It is, of course, much more common (though far from universal) among homosexual men, but about a quarter of young married couples today are reported to try it from time to time. According to the Hunt survey, one out of every seven college men said they liked the experience. Some women are apparently able to enjoy orgasm when rectal penetration is combined with clitoral stimulation and the practice was enthusiastically endorsed by "J" in *The Sensuous Woman*. But pain is more likely than pleasure unless both participants are thoroughly relaxed. There is an obvious health hazard, especially if fingers or penis are later in contact with the vagina without careful washing. Many men as well as most women have strong aesthetic objections to anal intercourse, and the symbolic associations with humiliation and degradation are very hard to eliminate. It seems to me that in this practice, which has begun to gain a certain mystique through pornographic movies, there is a new danger of men and women feeling they should engage in an activity, even though it is offensive to them, because their liberalism or their sexuality is thought to depend on it. And that strikes me as the antithesis of freedom and of mutuality.

If some, at least, of the expressions of mutual affection and intimacy that I have touched on briefly are enjoyed first, the experience of intercourse (if it turns out to be suitable in a relationship) is much more likely to be satisfying to both partners. If a couple are used to enjoying each other's bodies in a variety of ways, and if intercourse is the last of a whole series of mutually desired experiences, rather than a target or a concession, orgasm for the woman is much more likely—whether in vaginal penetration or by manual stimulation before, after or during intercourse. Initial failure by the man because of impotence or premature ejaculation will be less likely. If intercourse is part of a growing together rather than a challenge to be met, problems such as a lack of lubrication or vaginal pain can be discussed with understanding rather than becoming possible causes of embarrassment, disappointment, or recrimination. The fact that the woman may be at a stage of her menstrual cycle at which she is less able to respond can be taken into account. A common reason for a woman's failure to find intercourse satisfying—uncertainty about her partner's emotional involvement or his lack of concern for her pleasure—can be excluded. And finally, adequate steps can be taken to avoid pregnancy. If intercourse occurs in conditions of relaxation when there is no urgency to perform, the use of contraceptives can be incorporated into the process of lovemaking and their effectiveness will be a matter of mutually shared concern.

Of course, there's no way to guarantee that the most sincere attempt at sexual mutuality will result in a satisfying or long-lasting relationship. There will be disappointment and pain even with the best will in the world. One of the unavoidable things about sex is that two people, however responsive to each other, seldom develop their personal and physical involvement at the same tempo. Most people go through experiences in which one becomes more deeply committed than the other. Sometimes, with patience, the imbalance rights itself eventually, but often the outcome is tension and eventual separation. You can't be sexually intimate with another human being, whether intercourse is involved or not, without the possibility of wounding or being wounded. But surely the pain and disillusion arising when an honest relationship is terminated is quite different from what may follow a situation of sexual exploitation.

It is one thing to find that someone with whom you have shared a sensitive discovery of sexual pleasure cannot continue that exploration. It is a far more damaging experience to discover that someone who declared affection or love never really felt it. It is one thing to share your body with somebody in the course of a mutually shared development. It is quite another thing to do so under cultural pressure, on the basis of phony assurances, or to achieve some social benefit. It is one thing to explore the pleasures of sex as part of a fully human relationship: it is something else to treat one's genitals or those of a partner as a mere subject of curious experimentation divorced from the feeling, thinking, relating self. The superficial, coercive, impersonal alternative may well leave a heritage of guilt, repugnance, or self-contempt. Separation following an open relationship, while still painful, involves no lowering of mutual respect or self-esteem and may, in the long run, be a positive contribution to sexual and emotional growth.

eleven:

HOMOSEXUALITY

To Paul

I share your distress at the way your friend John has been treated by some of the other men in the dorm because they suspect him of being gay. You and I have talked freely enough about homosexuality to be able to approach the matter rationally, but few people are able to do so even today. You have to remember that the first Gay Liberation protest took place only a few years before you were born, and a California poll as recently as 1977 found that in that rather liberal state less than half the population advocated public approval or acceptance of a homosexual lifestyle. Although there are vocal Gay Liberation groups on many large campuses, the majority of homosexual students remain silent and frightened of detection. Indeed, smaller or more conservative college campuses may be among the most repressive places in the country. Grace and Fred Heckinger, after spending four months in extensive interviewing on campuses throughout the country during 1977, concluded that for a student to be homosexual is almost as much a disadvantage as it was thirty years ago. A survey conducted in a human sexuality class in 1977 showed that 72 percent of the men disapproved of homosexuality.

You have to remember that, although the law is changing and penalties are not often enforced, homosexual acts between consenting adults are still illegal in twenty-five states, and some voices on the extreme right have been calling for reintroduction of the death penalty—a punishment that was technically provided in the criminal codes of England and Scotland until a century ago! More to the point, some state legislatures have recently considered proposals to make *sympathy* for homosexuals justification for loss of employment; the U.S. immigration authorities decided in 1980 to continue to deport aliens who voluntarily declare their homosexuality; and in June 1981 the House of Representatives voted to bar the Legal Services Corporation from pressing cases involving homosexual rights. "To be a homosexual in our society," says Dennis Altman, "is to be constantly aware that one bears a stigma . . . [to be] part of a minority feared, disliked, and persecuted by the majority." Such deeply-rooted antagonism can only arise from some profound source.

As with many of our cultural standards, the rejection of homosexuals was originally expressed in religious terms. Jewish law vigorously condemned the "waste" of semen by homosexuals because nonreproductive sex was thought to threaten the maintenance of the race. The dramatic story of the destruction of Sodom in Genesis, chapter nineteen, was later interpreted to illustrate the divine punishment of homosexual behavior, although originally it probably had no sexual connotations. Christian teaching adopted this reading of the Sodom story with enthusiasm to support its rejection of all sexual practices not directed to reproduction. Medieval theologians taught that any ejaculation except into the vagina was unnatural, and subject to even more severe penalties than adultery or rape. (My personal view is that in thus singling out homosexuality and masturbation, celibate priests were punishing themselves for the sexual indulgence that most threatened their own vows.) But except in rigidly conservative groups these ideas are no longer influential and few college students condemn homosexuals for conscious religious reasons.

Another popular excuse for condemning homosexuality has been the conviction that it is a psychological disorder. I find it hard to take this seriously, since my homosexual friends have been among the most mature, sensitive and responsible people I have known. But probably because homosexuals suffer from emotional conflicts more than heterosexuals, in proportion to their numbers—largely due to the way society treats them, psychotherapists for years regarded homosexuality as a sickness in itself. Interestingly, however, Sigmund Freud specifically denied that it constituted a neurosis, and regular personality tests applied to homosexuals have been found to show the same range of patterns as those of heterosexuals. In the mid-1970s the American Psychiatric Association, by a substantial majority, endorsed a decision to delete homosexuality from its list of mental disorders. But even if it *were* a sickness, this would hardly explain the intensity with which so many men react to homosexuals. If your peers just thought John was emotionally ill their response would surely be more one of sympathy and support than of abhorrence and rejection!

It may be that some of them share the popular misconception that homosexuals are a danger to young boys—a fear that arouses public turmoil whenever a school teacher is found to be gay, or whenever a case of homicide involving homosexual seduction makes the headlines. But such anxieties are unfounded. In the first place, there is no reason to think that homosexuals are any more interested than heterosexuals in sex with children. In the second place, the average child (being heterosexually-oriented) is in no way liable to be "tainted" by contact with a homosexual adult, even if that person initiates sexual contact. Finally, the number of boys attacked by homosexual psychotics is much smaller than the number of girls abused and raped by heterosexual men (including their fathers). But I doubt, in any case, whether these considerations are present in the thinking of your dorm-mates when they react to John. I suspect they are motivated by deeper sexist anxieties, by irrational repugnance at male-with-male sexual intimacy, and by prejudiced ignorance about how people come to be homosexual.

The only explanation that seems to me to do justice to the persistence and strength of anti-homosexual feeling in our culture (and I lay no claim to originality in the idea) is that it represents a basic challenge to the male's self-image of superiority and power. In early patriarchy sexual activity between two males was probably interpreted as the submission by one man to another, the humiliation of a member of the male sex by adoption of the role of the female, the contradiction of masculine supremacy and a degradation to the level of womanhood. This view is explicit in Roman and early Christian thought. The false assumption that homosexual men are by definition effeminate, given to transvestism, characterized by lisping speech and limp wrists and that such "feminisms" are to be expected of males who have sex with men, reflects the same prejudice. Boys have been frightened to give expression to their feelings for fear of being thought "queer." Those of slight physique or artistic temperament have been ridiculed as "sissies" and have suffered quite unnecessary fears of being gay. On the other hand lesbians have never been persecuted with equal virulence and men who find male homosexual behavior repugnant often enjoy thinking of or watching women making love to each other. Both facts are explained by the basic (now often subconscious) objection to male subordination: for a women to obtain sexual satisfaction from another woman involves no disordering of the sexual hierarchy. There is no reason to feel contempt for a woman who "acts like a woman"—because this is to be expected of inferior beings!

I am always struck by the fact that whenever that excellent movie *Sunday, Bloody Sunday* is shown on our campus, an audible shock wave passes through our generally sophisticated student audience when the two male lovers first meet and kiss each other. Some deep nerve of disgust is touched by the sight of two men enjoying physical sexual contact. Despite our widespread cultural emphasis on the appeal of male physique, that attraction is associated with athletics and heterosexual behavior. In the first, the male body is celebrated because of its ability to surpass others in contest; in the second, it is celebrated as the proper object of admiration and desire—by women. For a man to find sensual pleasure in contact with a male body is for him to abandon the traditional role of competitor and superior, and to adopt the sexual response that is appropriate—to women. Sexual pleasure between males is thus quite irrationally repudiated by a culture that in every other form increasingly celebrates the erotic.

The same phenomenon is reflected in the current male attitude to anal intercourse, which is (quite incorrectly) assumed to be the universal sexual practice of homosexuals. It has become acceptable in heterosexual activity, often (to judge from both male and female accounts) despite the indifference or objections of the female partner. But the same physical act between two men is the subject for ridicule and disgust—sodomy has long been a term of abuse both for homosexual behavior and for anal intercourse. Yet the fact of the matter is that anal intercourse can apparently be an experience of sensitivity and love between homosexuals for whom vaginal connection is obviously impossible. One man wrote to Shere Hite: "After the act is completed what I remember most vividly and savor long afterward is the union, the tenderness, and the language that was established between my partner and myself. Just being inside of a man makes us a unit, and for that one moment of anal intercourse we are a complete ONE, emotionally as well as physically." It should not be impossible, though it may be difficult, for a heterosexual to respect such an expression of mutuality, *provided his sexual liberation includes freedom from the stereotype of male dominance and female inferiority.*

Rejection of the gay man as a pseudo-woman would not in itself, however, explain the paranoid anxiety and the homosexual baiting that goes on at colleges and elsewhere. It is the association of a second equally fallacious assumption with this sexist attitude that produces the vicious contempt your friend John is experiencing. The second part of the equation is the erroneous belief that homosexuality is contagious. This "prairie fire" myth implies that anyone is liable to be seduced into the gay ranks through contact or persuasion. Men who have experienced some homosexual attraction, however passing, often feel insecure about their sexuality. And it seems to be assumed, absurdly, that homosexual behavior is so clearly preferable that people will enlist in droves if they only learn about its pleasures. The very foundations of the social order are felt to be threatened by decline if homosexuality is permitted. Throughout history heretics and noncomformists of all types have been suspected of homosexual leanings. The word "bugger" is derived from the name of a medieval religious sect, the Bogomils of Bulgaria. In the present political climate we shall no doubt soon be told that the Russians are planning to destroy our manhood by supporting gay rights, despite the fact that communist society is even more anti-homosexual than ours.

As you can tell, I find this paranoia about homosexuality difficult to take seriously. In part this is, again, due to my own experience. As you know, I was sexually initiated at the age of twelve by a gay schoolmaster at the preparatory school I attended in England, then I spent all my adolescent years in another strictly male public (i.e. private) school, and went on to five years at Cambridge where, in those days, contacts with the few carefully segregated women students was almost nil. If anyone could be guided into adult homosexuality by pressure or indoctrination, I would surely have been: indeed if the idea that homosexuality is learned in adolescence were true, the proportion of gays in England would be far higher than in other nations—which it is not.

The very term "homosexual" is in need of clarification. Judd Marmor, one of the most respected authorities in a highly complex field, gives this definition in an invaluable book he recently edited: "One who is motivated in adult life by a definite preferential erotic attraction to members of the same sex and who usually (but not necessarily) engages in overt sexual relations with them." Note that by this definition homosexual experiences in adolescence (enjoyed, according to Kinsey, by one boy out of every three), or in circumstances (such as prison or military service) where contacts with females are impossible do not constitute evidence of homosexuality. Marmor also excludes those who choose homosexual partners only occasionally. Kinsey pointed out that there is an unbroken scale between those with exclusively heterosexual adult experience at one end and those with exclusively homosexual experience at the other end. The term "bisexual" is frequently used to describe all those within the two extremes, but this is misleading if it suggests that all of them are equally attracted by either sex. Although there may be some of whom this is true (Masters and Johnson suggest the term "ambisexual" for them), Marmor and others think that the great majority have a basic *preference*—though some heterosexuals enjoy homosexual partners occasionally and vice versa.

What, then, causes a person to be preferentially homosexual in adulthood? (I'm speaking of males here, although as you know the term includes women.) Here the experts disagree. The idea, once popular, that homosexuals are genetically distinguishable from heterosexuals is now largely abandoned. The possibility that variations in hormonal influences in the womb constitute a *predisposing* (though not determining) factor in at least some instances is widely recognized. But early childhood experiences, parental attitudes and cultural expectations are all thought to play a significant role. Poor family relationships in early childhood seem to be correlated with homosexual development, though this is not either a necessary or an inevitable precondition. The important thing, however, is that there is virtual agreement that, whatever the individual factors responsible, *a homosexual preference is established by the age of six or seven*. An individual with such a preference can choose whether to engage in homosexual acts or not. He may choose to seek and perhaps to acquire heterosexual orientation but *nobody chooses initially to become a homosexual*. To blame someone for this condition is unfair and ignorant.

For the same reason, it is absurd to fear that homosexuals will succeed in persuading large numbers of the population to share their way of life. This phobia is a product of the perennial tendency of a society to make scapegoats of any group it cannot understand, and it manifests itself particularly at times of cultural crises. In the past we treated any other species that *looked* threatening as natural enemies to be eliminated—until the ethologists taught us that aggressive looks or sounds from other animals are often not precursors of aggressive action. Rural people used to attribute all sorts of seductive powers to the inhabitants of big cities. Anti-semitism has been fed by a need to blame some distinguishable group for economic or natural disasters. Today those who are fearful of the future like to pick on gay liberation and warn that spreading homosexuality is a threat to our society. Some of the more vocal gay leaders sometimes sound as if they are out to proselytize, though strictly they are only concerned, rightly, for the termination of unjust laws by which they have been oppressed. In fact the percentage of homosexuals in the population remains quite steady: at most five to ten percent of adult males engage more or less exclusively in homosexual acts and perhaps the same number, in addition, engage only occasionally in homosexual acts. Evolutionary biological factors seem to ensure that heterosexual behavior remains the common preference. In the many societies that accept homosexuality without punishment or ostracism, it is less likely to become an exclusive preference than in cultures where homosexual activity is condemned. Indeed, our rigid distinction between male and female roles, with the excessive demands it places on boys to be dominant sexually, is thought by many to contribute to homosexual identification.

Sexual freedom must, surely, include the right to respond, subject to mutual consent and the normal considerations of privacy, to the sexual desires with which one is equipped. Imagine how you would feel if there were a law against your having any physical intimacy with your girlfriend! How would you respond to cultural pressures that told you it would be healthier or more mature or more Christian if you only dated *men?* How would it be to have to keep your private meetings with Ann a secret from your roommate and to have to pretend to join enthusiastically in homosexual locker-room talk? Try to help the guys in the dorm to grasp the situation of someone who has never *chosen* to love men, but who finds himself unaroused by women.

At the same time, I think you ought to encourage John to get some professional help with his sex life—particularly because he seems to have some uncertainty about his present orientation. Provided he receives competent, nonjudgmental counseling (your health service may offer it or at least know where to go) he stands to gain either way. If John is, in the terms I have used, a preferential homosexual, he may benefit from psychiatric help in several ways. First, he seems to need support in accepting himself as he is and freeing himself from the sense of guilt and inadequacy with which he has been burdened. Secondly, he may suffer from some sexual dysfunction like impotence which can, according to Masters and Johnson, be as effectively treated in homosexuals as it can in heterosexuals. But most important of all, he may need help in developing deep, mutual sexual relationships in a homosexual setting. For a variety of reasons male homosexuals can get caught up in a pattern of promiscuous sexual activities (though in that, of course, they are not different from some heterosexuals). Some seem to be driven by an obsessive neurotic search for purely impersonal sex, perhaps because they have so internalized the guilt that society lays on them for their "unnatural" desires, that they seek release in the most anonymous circumstances possible. We have made it so difficult for homosexuals to develop continuing relationships that many abandon the effort or never attempt it. The problem of integrating two personalities may be greater for two men than it is for a man and a woman. But what most homosexuals want, as shown by a survey in *Psychology Today* (March 1981), is a close and loving relationship with one special person. Here are two moving statements quoted by Hite: "My deepest longings are to find someone to form a lifelong, loving, give-take relationship based on love, trust, companionship and understanding." "My deepest longings are to find the person who fulfills me. Who I fulfill. With whom I find and can share the beauty I have seen. Someone I can cherish. Someone who builds me up when I am down."

With increasing social acceptance, this hope is being fulfilled for more and more gay men and their relationships are often as long-lasting and as rich as those of heterosexual married couples. Indeed there are those who argue that the relations of members of the same sex can be more truly mutual than those of heterosexuals. "I think that in gay relationships there is more of a sharing of power in the sexual encounter than there tends to be in heterosexual relationships," said one homosexual. Interestingly enough a Catholic moral theologian, John J. McNeill, has suggested that homosexual love, because it is free of the heterosexual role images, perhaps has a better chance to be genuinely interpersonal. And Masters and Johnson observed that homosexuals were markedly less genital and goal-oriented in their lovemaking, that they evinced much more concern for the satisfaction of their partners than did heterosexual males, and that they showed more sensitive understanding of their partner's erotic responses.

But finally, it's important for John to find out whether his dissatisfaction with his sexual life is due to the fact that he is not irrevocably committed to homosexual relationships. The fact that he is not responsible for his present orientation and cannot be blamed for it does not necessarily mean that he cannot, with proper therapy, adapt to heterosexual behavior. Nor, incidentally, does the fact that he *may* be able with proper help to make such a choice means that he can certainly, or that he can be blamed if he remains homosexual. Sexual freedom means not only freedom to be homosexual, if that is your destiny, it means freedom to choose the alternative if that option is open and if you wish to. Much as I applaud the accomplishments of gay liberation in achieving civil rights for homosexuals, I think that by urging students to "come out" and declare themselves once and for all they may be doing some a disservice.

Many students are unnecessarily anxious about their sexual orientation. This may be because of adolescent homosexual experiences, because the life of academic pursuits seems less manly than other ones, because of an unfortunate heterosexual experience, or because for the first time they are aware of the homosexual option. This self-doubt may result in a panic-stricken rush to join a gay group where, at least, there is acceptance and support. But a premature decision to come out can only lead to further confusion and pain. The Sarrels, from their experience at Yale, suggest that even for men who are definitely gay, coming out at college can expose them to sexual demands for which they are not yet ready.

As I've said, a person's homosexual inclinations are established in early childhood; but the intensity of those inclinations and their finality may depend on the extent to which there is any hormonally produced predisposition, and the manner and degree to which early experiences have contributed to the condition. It's as if a fork in the road is passed (quite unknown to the individual) by about age seven; but the breadth of the fork, the distance he may be separated from the heterosexual road, and the blocks set up to hinder a return to the other road vary from person to person. If a man has many satisfying homosexual experiences and establishes a valued pattern of homosexual social ties it may well be impossible, in practice, for him to move towards heterosexuality by the time he's in his twenties. Probably he will have no interest in doing so. On the other hand, if his homosexual experiences are mixed with heterosexual episodes that are enjoyable, if his social life is not closely tied to gay company and he strongly wants to live a heterosexual life, therapy may be effective. Masters and Johnson, using clinical methods involving a heterosexual partner, have recently reported much greater success with men, and women, seeking either "conversion" or "reversion" than had been thought possible. But their work was limited to the highly motivated and there remains some doubt as to how far they have been successful in modifying their clients' underlying erotic preference. At this juncture the most that can be said, for people in John's circumstances, is that if he seriously wants to change his orientation the possibility should be pursued. He should certainly resist the pressures (from both sides) to identify himself prematurely with the gay movement; by doing so he may close off the heterosexual alternative unnecessarily—and no responsible homosexual spokesman would encourage him to do that.

In the final analysis what matters is not whether a person lives his adult life as a homosexual or a heterosexual. What matters is that in his sexual relationships, of either kind, he has the freedom from guilt and fear that is essential to the growth of true mutuality. What matters is that his sexual behavior is the expression of a strong, integrated and fulfilling personal life. If our society is increasingly to make this freedom possible for homosexuals, the college campus should be in the forefront of knowledge, imagination and openness.

twelve:
LESBIANISM

To Jane

Since you're rash enough to ask me, I have to say that I think your roommate is making a mistake if she declares herself a lesbian and joins the women's liberation group because she was so miserably and inexcusably treated by her boyfriend. I say this at the risk of being misunderstood; but what I've written in earlier letters makes it clear, I hope, that I'm thoroughly in sympathy with women's protests against the patriarchal oppression that identifies having sex only with heterosexual intercourse.

A second clarification: my reaction to Donna's plan has nothing to do with condemnation of lesbians, or of her for admitting lesbian interests. Since lesbian sexual activity doesn't involve the discharge of semen or the acceptance by a male of a (supposedly) inferior, passive role, female homosexuals have been persecuted with less virulence than males—perhaps the only advantage women have enjoyed as a result of being regarded as the second sex! The fact that the percentage of female homosexuals is much smaller (most authorities agree in estimating it as half that of males) and the fact that our culture accepts the idea of women expressing their feelings physically probably explains why lesbians are better able to avoid public attack. But the hostility is deep. Many men resent the idea that women can be sexually satisfied without their help. Because our society rewards the woman who finds sexual satisfaction with men, heterosexual women all too often despise their lesbian sisters. Like some men, they may feel threatened by anxiety about their own adolescent homosexual experiences or by occasional feelings of physical attraction to members of their own sex. As one of our students bitterly expressed it: "Lesbians as lovers of women are obviously sick, aren't they? Because they don't love men. What could be more deviant than a women who didn't want to be fucked by a man (literally and figuratively)? And what can one say for a woman who shuns the obviously superior companionship and advice of men?"

The origins of female homosexuality, like those of male homosexuality, are complex. A true lesbian probably has her sexual orientation established for her by the age of six or seven as a result of early childhood experience and because of prenatal hormonal factors. By a true lesbian I mean a woman whose primary erotic attraction, *as an adult*, is to other women. I exclude those (the great majority of women) who have teenage crushes, occasional erotic attraction to a woman, or homosexual experiences only when isolated from males. According to Marcel Saghir and Eli Robins, lesbians are more likely than heterosexual women to exhibit tomboyish behavior in childhood, to lack close contact with a mother, and to engage in manual or oral genital stimulation with female partners in their teens or early twenties. It's important to remember that *these are not characteristic of all lesbians, and their existence does not necessarily mean that a woman is a lesbian*. If a woman does have a homosexual preference it is not a "perversion" that is willfully chosen, but the natural expression of a sexual identity for which it is absurd to blame or condemn anyone.

Let me finally emphasize that my hesitations about Donna's plans do not arise from any desire to discourage those who are fully convinced of their lesbian orientation from "coming out." There's no doubt that for some women a preference for female sexual partners is established and clear by the time they reach college, and it seems to me tragic that it is often so difficult for them to acknowledge this and discover others who share their preference. The following moving expressions of anguish and loneliness by women students are not atypical. "I wish so desperately that I could discuss this openly but maybe the time will come. I'm gay—and at college that has to be one of the most difficult things to be. . . . All I ask is this: be sensitive to it. Don't be predisposed. . . . One day I hope I can put my name to a letter like this but at this point, I think it would be downright foolishness. It is not that I am ashamed, but I would be risking an alienation that I am not willing to accept." "It seems ironic that at my very conservative high school I could find a female lover, yet here I know of no one else, man or woman, who is gay. . . . Is this because I've had the rare yet dubious honor of being the only homo in residence? . . . Openly affirming one's gayness here is slow social suicide. . . . I feel alone, isolated, not able to enjoy a social life to its full potential." If Donna feels like that I think she owes it to herself to make her gayness known. On the other hand at schools like yours, where there are vocal gay liberation organizations, there may be an opposite danger. Because of past oppression and the sense of being a persecuted minority, there is an understandable tendency to put pressure on all those who *think* they may be gay to identify themselves publicly. Experienced student advisors sometimes have to discourage women from prematurely announcing themselves as gay because of the social problems such a declaration involves and the possibility that it may cut them off from relationships with men that might yet be fulfilling. One homosexual psychiatrist told Grace and Fred Heckinger: "My task is not to get gay students to come out but to hold them back at a time when it may be inappropriate."

My real problem with Donna's intention is that she seems to be linking her understandable desire to affirm her freedom as a woman, brought to a head by this guy's thoughtless treatment of her, with embracing lesbianism. Of course some women begin lesbian relationships when they have a series of disappointing or antagonizing experiences with men, and this may be the catalyst in bringing to full realization the preconditioning factors of childhood. One woman told Hite: "I am currently thinking of lesbianism as an alternative to abstinence, and to men in general, because they are not very liberated sexually or emotionally or in any other way, and I can't stand it any more." But it is another thing to generalize this experience and to propose the adoption of lesbianism as a convenient or even essential tool in the struggle for women's freedom. Janis Kelly, for example, claims that lesbian relationships alone can be free of oppression and that "a woman would be foolish to be entirely open and trusting with a member of the [male] class whose very status is founded on her debasement."

There are several reasons why this lesbian-liberation equation seems to me unfortunate. First, it ignores the fact that most women can't choose to prefer erotic satisfaction with other women—any more than most men can choose to prefer sex with other men. Thus to lay on those interested in the woman's movement an obligation to change their sexual preference is to deprive the movement of the support of many heterosexual women. Secondly, it provides the opposition with a tool to use against the women's movement, since they can appeal to the popular dislike of gays and depict all liberated women as anti-male. Unfortunately, some lesbians have provided ammunition for this attack. As Betty Friedan has recently written: "We were diverted from our dream by a sexual politics that cast man as enemy and seemed to repudiate the traditional values of the family. . . . The very terms in which we fought for abortion, or against rape, or in opposition to pornography seemed to express a hate for men and a lack of reverence for childbearing." Finally, as Mary Daly and others have pointed out: "Doctrinaire insistence upon exclusive homosexuality fails precisely because it is not radical enough, for . . . it lends support to the notion that it *does* matter what the sex of your partner may be." As Daly insists, the goal of the women's movement must be not to establish women as oppressors in place of men, nor to aggravate the antagonism between the sexes that is so deeply embedded in our culture. The goal must be to bring to birth a new quality of interpersonal relationships, a society in which "*I-you* becomes the dominant motif, replacing insofar as possible the often blind and semi-conscious mechanisms of *I-It*, which use the Other as object." I'm sure that Donna does not intend to deny that principle, but I'm troubled by her elevation of what may turn out to be a temporary emotion, resentment against men, into a principle of political action.

In the last sentence I reveal my second reason for suggesting that you discourage Donna from coming out publicly just now: from what you have told me I doubt very much whether she is truly lesbian, and if she isolates herself from heterosexual experience she may unnecessarily narrow her personal development. It is true that some lesbians affirm the advantages of sex with women because they alone understand a woman's needs. Barbara Seaman quoted this example: "There are four advantages to lesbianism. First, a woman understands another woman's body so much better than a man can. Other women are better lovers. Second, women have prettier bodies, soft curves and smooth skin instead of bones and balls and hair in scratchy inappropriate places. Women are more cuddly and nicer to love. Third, women can't knock each other up. You don't have to spoil the beauty of the act messing around with birth control. You don't get frantic when your period is late. Fourth and most important, in a healthy lesbian relationship, you are equals as men and women in our society cannot yet be."

On the other hand, many women who are not lesbians suffer the kind of trauma to which Donna has been subjected, and eventually achieve sexual satisfaction in good mutual relationships with men. From the fact that she has, I gather, not only had heterosexual experiences in the past but has found them to be enjoyable and satisfying, my guess is that her present lesbian liaison is more rebound from her disastrous affair with Sam than the start of a pattern that will satisfy her permanently. There is, after all, another side to the argument that sexual partners of the same sex are more attuned to each other. The psychologist C.A. Tripp has argued that a certain tension is integral to creative personal interaction: "The benefits of a smooth togetherness are bought at the price of dwindling erotic tensions—a descent which can easily threaten the whole enterprise." I don't agree with some of the conclusions that Tripp draws from this point, but I think it contains a truth. Provided that the necessary heterosexual erotic attraction exists, and provided that dominance and submission have been replaced by mutuality, it seems to me that the differences of temperament and physiology brought by a man and a woman to a relationship may contribute to, rather than detract from its richness. If Donna concludes, after adequate experimentation and reflection, that she is lesbian, she most certainly should feel no embarrassment or shame about the fact. But if she prematurely restricts her freedom to have heterosexual relationships, she may deny herself the kind of experience in which she can most fully mature.

I am not denying for a moment that the decision to give conscious and/or public recognition to the fact that one is lesbian can be wonderfully liberating. Once free of pretence and false guilt, lesbian women are able to develop strong, supportive relationships together. The promiscuity that characterizes some male homosexuals is virtually unknown among females; cruising for casual sex, for example, is not part of the lesbian scene. Lesbians commonly succeed in combining love and sex in sensitive, fulfilling unions. Prolonged relationships are the norm more than the exception. All of which is a way of saying that whatever final path Donna takes there's no need for you to be anxious about her happiness. The only thing I do suggest you urge on her is that she should be sure before making public declarations.

thirteen:
RELIGION

To Paul

I'm glad to know that my earlier letter was helpful in
relieving your roommate of some of his guilt about
masturbation, but I think you will have more difficulty in
persuading him to modify his convictions about premarital
chastity. Indeed I'm not at all sure that you should try to
change his mind on this issue. It's true that the traditional
religious prohibition of intercourse before marriage has in the
past been asserted and accepted purely on authority, and in
the modern world this makes it difficult for most of us to take
it seriously. But ideas supported by bad reasons are not
necessarily false, and both you and David should know how
religious thinkers argue for preserving intercourse for
marriage. I'll try to put their position clearly, but before I do
so there are a number of facts you should bear in mind.

First, it's all too easy to blame religion for the existence of
cultural restraints on sexual freedom as if religion
represented an independent system of ideas imposed from
the outside on society. It is true that nowadays conservative
churches and synagogues hold to a rigid standard that most
students don't accept. But, as Clellan Ford and Frank Beach
concluded on the basis of studying 190 different cultures:
"No human society condones promiscuous or indiscriminate
mating. Every culture contains regulations that direct and
restrict the individual's selection of a sexual partner or
partners." And in virtually all societies these regulations

were originally supported by religious beliefs. Freud, despite his dismissal of religion as "illusion," was emphatic in arguing that some limits on sexual indulgence and the "sublimation" of the sexual urge (libido) into other creative channels was essential for the development of civilization. Thus even those of us who do not accept the traditional Western religious attitude to sex owe a great deal to it, and in many ways still live by its basic ideals. For example, the "commandment" I proposed to you earlier, "Don't Treat a Person as a Thing," was given rational formulation in the eighteenth century by Immanuel Kant, whose assumptions (as he freely acknowledged but modern philosophers tend to forget) were derived from his Christian background.

Secondly, the sexual attitudes of early Judaism were far less rigid than those of Christianity, and Jewish culture has never denied the proper place of sexual pleasure. The Hebrews were indeed the puritans of the ancient world, partly in reaction against the orgiastic fertility worship of the Canaanites, the original inhabitants of the "promised land." We owe a good deal to their rejection of sexual indulgence as an end in itself and their direction of energy into developing a richer, more progressive civilization. But, as David Feldman points out in his authoritative study of Jewish attitudes to birth control, Jews were *forbidden* to deny each other intercourse in marriage, and contraception in order to allow pleasure without reproduction was not condemned. Only Jews of strictly orthodox persuasion down-play the goodness of sex under the influence of later mystical ideas. Jesus appears to have been much less concerned with sex than with selfishness, less condemnatory of adultery than of self-righteousness. Recent studies have drawn attention to the fact that Jesus, if he was truly human, must have had sexual desires, and a Presbyterian theologian, William Phipps, has argued seriously (though not, I think persuasively) that as a rabbi he must have been married.

Unfortunately the Christian church, under Stoic and Neoplatonic influences, radically modified the healthy sexuality of Judaism and failed to follow Jesus in his treatment of women as equals with men. "It is the teaching on virginity which was a radical break from the Old Testament," says the Catholic scholar John Noonan. Bishops and theologians were soon teaching that intercourse in marriage, except for purposes of reproduction, was as wicked as adultery because such acts "befoul intercourse with pleasure." Homosexuals and prostitutes were denied communion throughout the middle ages even when they were dying. (The recent attempt by the Yale historian John Boswell to argue that Christian society was fairly tolerant of homosexuals until the thirteenth century is not convincing, though it is true that they were not actually executed until then!) It was not until the twentieth century that official Catholic teaching allowed that some pleasure during sex was without sin, and only within the last twenty years has the significance of sexuality as an essential and positive element in human life been recognized. Pope John Paul II has strongly affirmed "the personal dignity of the body and of sex," but since he also condemns artificial contraception as "unworthy of civilization," most people will find his reassurances unpersuasive.

A third point to remember is that the fundamentalist use of the Bible as a textbook to settle issues of sexual ethics is rejected as irrational by the great majority of religious thinkers. The Old Testament passage (Leviticus 20) used by fundamentalists to attack homosexuals contains equally strong condemnations of a child who curses his parents or a married couple who have intercourse during menstruation. If the Old Testament were taken literally women would not wear slacks, since this is prohibited in Deuteronomy 22; indeed, a Baptist minister was recently convicted of child neglect for spanking his daughter for breaking this "law." Both Catholic and Protestant scholars reject such simplistic nonsense. For example, an influential group of Catholic theologians under the chairmanship of Father Anthony Kosnik recently stated that "the Bible should not be seen as giving absolute prescriptions with regard to sex. Specific culturally conditioned instructions cannot claim validity for all time." The same group shared a widespread recognition that St. Paul's condemnation of homosexuals (in Romans 1) was based on his association of sexual excess with pagan idolatry, and that it is absurd to accuse all homosexuals of these faults. As a study prepared for the United Church of Canada in 1980 pointed out: "It goes without saying that to know a number of homosexual people at all well is to know that they exhibit no more conspicuous inclination to idolatry than is evident in all the rest of us."

The fact is that despite the unfortunate impression that rigid fundamentalism and traditional Catholicism represent religion, most lay members of churches and synagogues take a much more liberal view of sex, and many religious leaders and theologians recognize the values in the sexual revolution. A majority of Catholics in the United States do *not* believe that premarital sex is wrong, three out of four Catholic women in this country use contraceptive devices and almost as high a percentage of American priests do not consider their use a serious sin. Many of the major Protestant churches have come out strongly in favor of equal rights for homosexuals, and some of them have ordained known homosexuals to their ministries. According to "situation ethics" as formulated by the Episcopalian, Joseph Fletcher, the criterion by which the good or evil of any sexual behavior is judged is not a biblical text or an ecclesiastical tradition but conformity to the principle of love: thus in certain circumstances *any* act could be morally justified if it served the good of a person or of persons.

It remains true, however, that no church, as far as I know, has officially modified the ideal of premarital chastity. I don't myself think it is practicable or even desirable as a strict rule, but it has played an important role in our cultural history; it's not inconsistent with full respect for the good in sexuality, it's not based on some isolated text, and it deserves to be taken seriously because there are sensible reasons that can be

:105

advanced in its favor. Contemporary religious teachers defend premarital chastity not because they equate sex and reproduction or deny the proper place of pleasure in human life, but because they value marriage as a unique experience of interpersonal union and believe that the quality of married life depends, at least in part, on the special intimacy of intercourse being preserved for that relationship.

In coitus, it is suggested, two people discover for the first time what it means to be a whole person—male or female, and this experience should be enjoyed with the person with whom one is to share one's life. If you have intercourse with anyone else you exclude the possibility of sharing this unique bond with your wife or husband. A Protestant scholar, William Hamilton, put the point as effectively as anyone: "If it is true that sexual intercourse mediates a unique kind of personal knowledge, it is clear that a very special status must be given to the first experience of the sexual act. The first sexual experience is so overwhelming and so different from any other experience that it is better reserved as a means of symbolizing and giving meaning to marriage." Note that, strictly, this is an argument in favor of having intercourse only with the person you eventually marry, not in support of only having intercourse after a wedding ceremony. In medieval Catholic practice a couple who engaged in intercourse were not severely condemned if they then married. In Puritan England and America the fact that a bride was pregnant was no particular cause for embarrassment and was sometimes recorded in the parish register. And some contemporary Catholic moral theologians argue that "preceremonial intercourse" is not the same as premarital intercourse, and need not be a sin.

There is something to be said, it seems to me, for the view that extensive premarital sexual experience takes away from the strength of the bond that a married couple shares. Vernon Grant, a psychiatrist with no religious ax to grind, thinks that lack of exclusiveness reduces the sense of mutual respect and value. He quotes this comment by a young woman who was attracted to a man but doubtful about marrying him: "When I think of all those women it would be hard to have romantic thoughts about marrying him. I don't mean exactly that he is shopworn but that he has certainly been the opposite of hard to get. I can't think of him as having high standards of taste. It makes him a bit common somehow, and that would make a relationship with him a bit common too. I'm not trying to make any kind of magic out of sex. But I do think there ought to be something that sets one relationship apart from others if it really is different, and if it is to lead to marriage." Two Catholic authors, O'Neil and Donovan, argue that premarital intercourse can be the cause of suspicion, resentment and insecurity: "Sexuality by its very nature demands a certain exclusiveness, possessiveness and permanence. . . . Fidelity and the unquestioned trust of each spouse in the other's commitment to be faithful are necessary conditions of a happy marriage." In our world, of course, there is another side to it: the lack of any other experience may be an encouragement to postmarital adventures when society takes these so much for granted and offers so many opportunities.

At least I hope I have persuaded you that the decision to preserve one's virginity for marriage is not necessarily an immature one—on the contrary, the ability to defer immediate satisfaction for what is thought to be a greater future good is usually a sign of inner strength. The argument that the special intimacy of intercourse should be the distinctive expression and symbol of the special commitment of marriage is not one to be despised, and David has no need to apologize if this is his motive. At the same time I have to add that I personally think that the traditional religious position carries with it real dangers.

All too often an absolute restriction on intercourse masks an unhealthy, negative and repressive rejection of sexual pleasure that is due to a rigid religious upbringing. One student of mine had been taught in his Catholic school that any kissing before marriage that resulted in "reaction in the organs of regeneration" was illicit and dangerous. A Protestant marriage handbook published during the past few years warned against "any kind of sexual excitement" between an engaged couple. An Orthodox Jewish guide for youth that is still in use prohibits even holding hands before marriage. The result of such teaching and the attempt to avoid sex before marriage is the widespread incidence of what has been called "ecclesiogenic neuroses." Masters and Johnson reported that narrow religious orthodoxy was a major cause of sexual dysfunction and the most difficult to treat. Though the intention of the rule of chastity may be to strengthen marriage, it can have the opposite effect of sowing the seeds of marital disaster. A man or woman who has been taught to fear and avoid sex for years cannot suddenly acquire a new attitude as a result of the wedding ceremony. A Catholic woman wrote to *Commonweal* to say: "I was taught that heterosexual sex was for procreation, not pleasure (even in marriage), that sexual thoughts and behavior were lustful and a mortal sin. . . . I have discussed this subject of guilt with countless married Catholic women, and . . . our feelings of guilt toward sex are so deep and ingrained, that we can't even enjoy sex in marriage."

The trouble is that religious teaching about sex and marriage was developed in a world that no longer exists—except, perhaps, in Iran and Saudi Arabia. What mattered in marriage was not love but parenthood and permanence, the sexual satisfaction of women was of no importance, and pregnancy and VD were ever-present deterrents to premarital intercourse. People married much younger so that adolescent sexual needs were satisfied in a socially acceptable context. In our culture we have a totally different situation: mutual love is assumed to be an essential ingredient in marriage, pregnancy and VD no longer arouse serious fears (though they are real dangers), and many college students are already past the age at which sexual desire has reached a peak.

Today, sexual fulfillment and personal happiness are valued at least as much as strict fidelity, and the perpetuation of a marriage when these are lacking is no longer socially expected. Learning to relate with sensitivity in sexual intimacy (possibly including intercourse) may be a much better preparation for a sound and long-lasting marriage than preserving an intact hymen. A report prepared by the Rev. Richard Unsworth for a task force of the United Presbyterian Church made this illuminating comment: "In our time, a pattern of many intense but short-lived relationships may be a more ominous portent of unfaithfulness than the simple failure to come virginal to the marriage relationship. In fact, our culture could unwittingly erode the capacity for faithfulness in its young by disregarding the emotional and spiritual significance of various forms of sexual behavior, while simplistically maintaining the arbitrary standards of technical virginity."

Our fixation on intercourse as *the* forbidden act has the unhappy consequence of forcing many young people to get married because they can't wait any longer to enjoy their sexual relationship fully, and society, while encouraging, or at least allowing "everything but," requires of them a formal license before they actually sleep together. It is notorious that such early marriages end more often and more quickly in divorce. Would it not be better to postpone marriage until economic or educational circumstances made it viable, and to accept intercourse earlier as part of a responsible relationship? The quality and permanence of marriage would often be improved if a couple, instead of concentrating their energies on avoiding intercourse, could get to know and evaluate each other as full persons. If your sexual contacts are limited to brief occasions, attention is easily focused on the physical excitement to the exclusion of concern about compatibility in other respects. Successful erotic response can be mistakenly taken to imply mutuality of interests and a couple may find that once the honeymoon is over they have nothing in common but sex. One young mother stated that as a result of intercourse before marriage she and her husband found that "by the end of our courtship, sex was a secondary consideration in our decision to marry. We weren't looking eagerly toward marriage so we could experience the 'ultimate in human response.' We knew sex as an expression of ourselves—sometimes gentle and sweet, sometimes painful and cruel, sometimes a passionate orgy, sometimes a retreat from reality, but always a new experience. . . . We would have enough adjusting to do as man and wife—at least we would be spared the sometimes frightening and harsh experience of exploring untapped sexual responses."

Whether this would be true for David, only he can judge and only time can tell. The issues are so complex that there is no simple answer to the question, "Does premarital intercourse help or hinder marriage?" However, as even Kinsey realized (and he was hardly sympathetic to religious scruples), every individual has to follow his deepest convictions and so long as David is persuaded that premarital intercourse is morally wrong he should avoid it, or he may risk internal conflicts and problems if he does marry.

fourteen:
LOVE

To Jane

I can well understand the problem you have deciding
whether you love Jim or not. One woman student was
quoted recently as saying, "It gets to be hard to try to sort
out whether you're having a casual relationship, or if you're
infatuated, or if you think you're in love. It takes a lot of your
mental time." Is love something you "fall into" or something
you do? Do you "make love" or does it sweep you away? The
ambiguity was delightfully expressed by Lois Gould in her
hilarious but bitter novel, *Such Good Friends.* Fantasizing
about a sexual relationship, Julie imagines herself explaining
the situation to an inquiring judge: "We made love, Your
Honor. He didn't have any and neither did I. So we made
some. It was good."

In recent years I notice an increasing hesitation among
college students to talk about love in relation to sex. In an
entirely understandable reaction against the unreality of our
cultural obsession with romantic love, people of your
generation prefer to talk about "affection." A woman told
George Lower that formerly she would have said that
intercourse was acceptable only for those in love, but now
thinks "It is all right for those who simply share affection.
The reason for this change is that I'm not sure what love is."
Affection seems to imply personal concern, mutual
openness, trust and lack of coercion—without the suggestion
of unqualified commitment and heady devotion that "love"

conveys. Hite quotes men who use words like "blinded," "disorientation," "foolishness," "illusion," "out of control," "sick," "crazy," "mental illness" to express their fear of love.

Romantic love has come under fire from the psychologist Lawrence Caster in an article entitled "This Thing Called Love is Pathological": "To the extent that love fosters dependency, it may be viewed as a deterrent to maturity. . . the person who seeks love in order to obtain security will become, like the alcoholic, increasingly dependent on this source of illusory well-being." The very idea that love is something you "fall into" suggests a loss of self-direction and overwhelming addiction that reasonable people naturally shy away from. A typical example is the young man who declared: "If I lost her I'd sort of die, I'd go mad. . . . She's all I live for, all I work for. . . . I can't go wrong with her." Stendahl put it with acuity: "Even the most prudent person, from the very moment he or she is in love, ceases to see an object as it really is. He underrates his own advantages and overestimates the slightest favor of the beloved creature."

A second vigorous attack has been mounted by some feminists. Germaine Greer wrote movingly about "the wretched cant" of love, "masking egotism, lust, masochism, fantasy under a mythology of sentimental postures, a welter of self-induced miseries and joys, blinding and masking the essential personalities in the frozen gestures of courtship, in the kissing and dating and the desire, the compliments and the quarrels which vivify its barrenness." What she had in mind, justifiably, is the way in which our culture has deluded women into a pattern of sexual response which has been largely male-dominated. Women have been discouraged from accepting their own sexuality as a good in itself: sex is only respectable, so girls have learned, when it is an expression of love. But love involves a lover, a male, and thus sex is justified only when Prince Charming appears. When he speaks the magic word, affirming *his* love, then the sleeping princess is aroused and responds, according to the script. Unfortunately, it transpires all too often that he was only mouthing stage lines and she awakens to find herself alone. It's not surprising that many modern women think love a four-letter word that is inconsistent with sexual and personal freedom. Love all too often means possessiveness rather than mutuality. "The terms of such passion," wrote Greer, "are all negative. 'I never wanted anyone but you: you're the only woman I've ever loved,' is taken as sufficient justification for undisputed possession. Because the lover cannot live without his beloved she must remain with him even against her will. . . . As long as the beloved stays she may be treated with great generosity but once she leaves she is an object of hatred and reprisal."

There's a great deal of truth in these attacks on romantic love. Even the most sincere of us has difficulty (as you have right now) in deciding what love is and what kind of relationship exists between us and someone who attracts and fascinates us. Joseph Conrad once remarked that "no man fully understands his own artful dodges to escape from the grim shadow of self-knowledge," and that's especially true of sexual passion: it's awfully easy to persuade yourself that something admirable and substantial called love exists when there's nothing there but instinctual infatuation. People are propelled into marriage by this logic: "Since I'm so sexually excited by this person I must be in love, since I'm in love I can or must have intercourse, since I've had intercourse (or want to have it) I ought to get married, and since we love each other any problems that happen to surface now can be resolved after the wedding."

It's not surprising that so many of your peers, who have often suffered the consequences of parental marriage based on this nonsense, want nothing to do with it. Yet it seems to me a tragedy if you become so suspicious of love that you miss what there is in it of value—simply because you have been sold a shoddy bill of goods under the title romantic love. Provided it is recognized as a possible starting point and not as an end, as an elementary introduction and not as a mature conclusion, "falling in love" can be a joyful, liberating, ecstatic experience that gives new meaning to life and transforms one's world. A study by a psychiatrist, William Kephart, found no evidence that romantic love is indicative of a neurotic personality and three out of four people think love has made their lives happier, whatever its complications. That most women think love important in a sexual relationship is well-established, but it is becoming clear that more and more men, despite their upbringing and their hesitation to acknowledge the fact, value it deeply. The 1981 *Playboy* survey found that its readers consistently prized love more than money, work or sex. Men in Hite's sample recognized that love needs cultivation but thought that it could start as an intense, emotional attraction: "The initial infatuation isn't really love, but without it, I don't think love can really develop and mature. To use a bad metaphor—it's like fine wine—age and time will mellow, smooth and mature the vintage—but the grapes have to be right at the start for something really special to result."

The Greeks had three words for love, as you may know: *eros* which means desire, the love for that which attracts us and fills a need (not specifically a sexual need—according to Plato it is *eros* that draws the soul to seek knowledge of the eternal Forms); *philia* which means friendship, the love of companions, of the community, or of one's country; and *agape*, the word that represents self-giving—the nearest modern equivalent perhaps is altruism. There has been a tendency to regard these as quite distinct: certainly one or the other often predominates and even excludes another; but I believe they can coexist. For example, any deep friendship probably has an erotic element in it. Sexual love, *eros*, can lift a person out of his individual self-centeredness and involve self-giving concern for another—at least a beginning of *agape*. Barbara Seaman calls this "transcendent sex" because, she says, "It is an almost mystical experience of renewal, where body and soul seem to be perfectly integrated, existence is given meaning and immortality is somehow affirmed." The

114:

result is that the man or woman is "more spontaneous, more open, more confident, more loving, more purposeful, and more peaceful." I suggest that satisfying, mature love depends on the existence in both partners of some combination of all three—erotic attraction, shared interests and loyalties, and the ability sometimes to sacrifice one's own preference or advantage for the other person. It usually begins in our society with *eros* and grows to include *philia* and *agape*. In other cultures a relationship starting with *philia* or *agape* often develops into *eros*. In our rather peculiarly Western tradition of starting with *eros* it's virtually impossible at first to distinguish the beginning of real love from merely physical infatuation. If you don't find your feelings for Jim beginning to show the characteristics of *philia* and *agape*, you should ask yourself whether you love him in a way that can be the basis for an ongoing relationship. If your attraction is purely erotic you will probably soon tire of each other.

Philia is a vital component of adult love. However much love may begin as sexual passion and physical attraction, it withers and dies if a couple share no mutual interests beyond that of erotic satisfaction. This certainly doesn't mean that every activity has to be undertaken in harness—excessive togetherness can be smothering—but that each needs to be interested in what the other does. The ability to discuss and disagree about politics, art, religion, or literature and a readiness to explore new fields together are vital. A sense of humor, the capacity to kid each other, pure enjoyment of each other's company, freedom to share secret hopes and fears (without expecting unqualified endorsement)—all the subtle bonds that make for good friendship are, it seems to me, integral to love. They may not all be present in bloom from the start, for love takes time to mature, but if the seeds of *philia* are not present you should recognize that your feelings for Jim probably have limited prospects. "If our relationship is a progressive thing, not merely a static achievement," says Anthony Storr, "we may approximate to a stage in which, because each fulfills the other's need, each is also treated as a whole person by the other. Whereas formerly two people in love served only to complete what each felt to be lacking—now two people confront each other as individuals."

Agape is being able to admire and respect another without the delusions of romantic love. It seeks to give *to* the other, which by definition implies that the beloved is not already perfect and sufficient and that the lover has something of value to share. After all, the exhortation "love your neighbor as yourself" is about *agape*, and it doesn't mean "love your neighbor *instead* of yourself." As I pointed out in an earlier letter, without self-love or self-respect true love is impossible, since there is nothing of worth in the self to offer to another. In romantic love the lover projects on the other person the ideal qualities that he or she would like to have: thus criticism of the beloved cannot be tolerated because it would destroy the illusion of an idealized self. Mature love is able to acknowledge the inadequacies as well as the good qualities of the self and of the beloved; at the same time it is able, as Abraham Maslow suggested, to perceive hidden potentialities in the other because insights are heightened in love.

It is important not to confuse this ability to perceive the true potential of the person we love with an intention to interfere or to impose our will on him or her. Nothing is more disastrous than a relationship in which one partner sets out to save the other from himself or herself. The psychoanalyst Erich Fromm described love as "the active concern for the life and growth of that which we love," a concern that finds expression in care, responsibility, respect, and true knowledge of the other. Milton Mayeroff, a philosopher, suggests the word "caring" to represent *agape*, and defines it as "helping him grow and actualize himself"—not imposing my direction but allowing growth to guide my response. *Agape* does not pretend that all is perfect, and seeks to share with (and receive from) the beloved without any intention to mold him or her in its own image. True lovers do not become carbon copies of each other but rather more autonomous, more complementary, more able to give and to receive.

Of course, the erotic element remains significant even when it no longer occupies the primary role it had in romantic attraction. And one characteristic of romantic love that commonly persists in adult love is a concern for sexual exclusiveness. There are those who maintain that a mature love should be untroubled by the sharing of intercourse with third parties. In so far as sexual exclusiveness is imposed on women but not on men, I agree that it is objectionable. It is surely sexist to expect women to be monogamous while allowing men to enjoy sexual variety if they so choose. Again, if a love relationship is *destroyed* by any infatuation or romantic attraction that disturbs its harmony, the strength of the relationship is called into question. I believe that love should be able to survive passing affairs. Mature couples can cope with such tensions creatively—provided, as is often the case, that a sexual diversion does not threaten the primary commitment of *agape* and *philia*. But it seems to me a new romantic unrealism to suppose that for most people love can be indifferent to the question of sexual exclusiveness, or indeed that in principle it should be. I am not arguing for the possessiveness of the romantic lover who is jealous of a partner's ocial relationships with a member of the other sex. I am suggesting that love usually needs to be confident that the ultimate sexual intimacy will not be shared with others. Students who are deeply in love or living together tend to be notably monogamous and distressed by concurrent affairs.

Open marriage seems to me an idea whose time has passed, since couples committed to the ideal of complete sexual tolerance seem to split up and regroup. I'm all for our society accepting communes and group marriage as alternative lifestyles, but it appears that they usually start from and lead to dyadic relationships. The *expectation* of fidelity, trust in consistency, and the presumption of mutual satisfaction seem to be integral to love for the great majority of people. The late Silvano Arieti suggested that for one partner to share intercourse with a third person inflicts an injury on the relationship because "to know the loved one had attempted to have a peak experience with somebody else is difficult to endure." It is interesting to note that an example of a highly egalitarian marriage contract published in *Ms* (June, 1981), which provided for a complete sharing of privileges and duties and for great independence in social life and careers, included this clause: "The parties freely acknowledge their insecurity about sexual relationships beyond the partnership. Therefore the parties agree to maintain sexual fidelity to each other."

fifteen:
LIVING TOGETHER

To Jane

If you decide to move in with Jim, it's okay with us.
Indeed it's becoming almost commonplace. It's estimated
that a quarter of all students live together for at least some
part of their college years. Four out of every five say they will
do so if the opportunity comes along. More than half report
that the experience is "very successful," and a majority (even
among those whose relationship has terminated) say they
would do it again with the same person. So you'd be in good
company and the chances are that you and Jim would
benefit. At the same time, I think you ought to be aware of
some of the problems that people have with the experiment.

Most couples decide to live together to share more time
without the hassle of separate rooms and upset roommates.
Despite the suspicions of many adults, the primary reason is
usually not sexual, and sometimes the people involved are
not even lovers. Eleanor Macklin, the leading authority on
student cohabitation, says that some couples live and sleep
together for several months before having intercourse. In
many instances, where students are allowed to make their
own living arrangements off-campus, economic
considerations play a part. But the primary rewards people
look for, as you do, are the growth of companionship, greater
intimacy, unpressured sex, and mutual self-discovery.
Living together doesn't involve the public finality of a marital
commitment, but it does make possible a balanced

relationship rather than a series of primarily sexual or romantic interludes. It's the informality of the situation that appeals to many, and that may explain some of its successes. When you're living with someone there's less pressure on you to make them over in your own image: if he or she does things that irritate you or exhibits qualities you don't appreciate, you can always take comfort in the fact that you're not tied to each other as you would be if you were married. On the other hand, this informality may be misleading. Most students don't decide to move in together as a result of a carefully thought-out decision: usually it starts with staying overnight for convenience, then keeping a few clothes in the closet, and finally discovering almost *post facto* that the move has been made. But the arrangement can very soon attain a status which makes separation extremely difficult, and what starts almost by accident can become a felt commitment, a hidden trap that springs silently and imperceptibly. The idea that cohabitation involves "no strings" is a fallacy. So I'm glad that you and Jim are talking seriously about what you're getting into before you decide.

The fact is that living together, as well as having some of the disadvantages of marriage, may involve some additional difficulties. For example, there is inevitably deception that can at times be embarrassing or can produce tension. You probably can't tell the school authorities or your professors. We have no objection to your plans, but I gather Jim's parents and family don't exactly approve—a situation in which half the students who cohabit today still find themselves, unfortunately. More serious, however, is the danger that you may isolate yourselves from your friends and cut yourselves off from social activities. You may be so anxious to cultivate your personal relationship (and perhaps under pressure to do so before the semester ends) that you fail to develop common or individual relationships on campus. A male student recently expressed some fear that this would happen to him and his partner: "Lots of times you see couples who get together, who do nothing, who spend their whole time together. They lose all the good friends they have—and just drop all the activities they are doing." Apart from the danger of becoming socially ingrown, you're liable to miss out on many of the opportunities for cultural expansion that college offers.

A further problem is that conflicting goals and traditional patriarchal discrimination may have even more serious consequences for a woman than they do in a traditional marriage. The woman still tends to get landed with the domestic chores, or a disproportionate part of them. If the relationship terminates you can only assert any legal rights through a court process, if then. And women are at greater emotional risk than men, since women are, according to the studies I have seen, much more likely than men to hope that living together will be a prelude to marriage. Even if they don't enter the arrangement with that in mind, they are more likely than many men to find the emotional bonds difficult to throw off. Ingrid Bengis, by no means a dependent or domesticated woman, discovered that her attachments to men usually deepened while their's lessened: "I didn't realize that sex made a difference . . . that it transformed everything, that for me and for most women, making love with a man several times created unpredictable bonds—which weren't broken by saying, 'This was a trial marriage for which the contract has expired.'"

In the light of all this Eleanor Macklin and many others doubt whether the commitment to living together in college is wise or beneficial. She thinks there is a tendency "to become overinvolved and to feel a subsequent loss of identity . . . and an over-dependency on the relationship." An experienced psychiatrist has suggested that "those who cohabit are gratifying personal imperatives but lack the psychological qualities to make the heterosexual bond durable." I believe you are sufficiently mature to make the experience a positive one, but I think you ought to consider the possible advantages of delaying a domestic commitment until you and Jim (or whoever it might be) are prepared to take the step of getting married. I know that marriage is a dirty word among many of your peers, and I certainly don't recommend it for many undergraduates; but I can't resist the opportunity to point out that marriage does potentially have some advantages as a way of living together. Oddly enough, although most students are understandably skeptical of marriage as they have observed it, the great majority still expect to marry eventually. Perhaps there's something to the conviction of those anthropologists who argue that pair bonding is part of our essential evolutionary genetic equipment. In any case, it is generally agreed that cohabitation does not replace marriage but only delays it. Nearly all of those who live together say they eventually plan to be married (though not necessarily to their present partner).

Of course, I'm not advocating the oppressive, patriarchal marriage that still comes to mind when the word is used. I've a lot of sympathy with those who have described marriage as a "wretched institution," as a "lethal gas chamber," as a "culturally approved neurosis," and as "domestic slavery." Nor am I about to give any assurance that marriage will be better for your generation, or that any particular marriage can be a guaranteed success. It is certainly not the right choice for some, and many people who get married would be better off if they remained single. On the other hand the high divorce rate (now one out of three) doesn't necessarily mean that marriage is a total disaster area. Indeed the increase in divorce rates may partly represent not the decline of marriage but a higher standard of expectation and the termination of unions that in the past would have been maintained as hell on earth. Women, in particular, are rightly in rebellion against an institution which has condemned them to subordination and frustration for so long. The fact is that good marriages depend on a combination of mutually compatible personalities, strong and growing love such as I described in my last letter, and—let's face it—a good deal of luck. A couple of years ago

I examined all the major studies of marital success and failure and concluded that they prove absolutely nothing at all—except that millions of people in this country think marriage the best thing that ever happened to them and millions of others think it the worst. So don't assume that your happiness is necessarily best served by choosing not to marry: given the right circumstances and the right partner it may one day prove to be a path to happiness and self-development that you would otherwise never discover. And I believe it's precisely the element in marriage—public commitment—that mere living together lacks, that is its strength. What you may think of as an undesirable restriction on freedom can contribute to the growth of love and to sexual fulfillment.

I would define marriage as *a freely chosen, public commitment as a means to growth in mutuality*. Today it is certainly your choice: neither satisfaction of your sexual needs, nor law, nor social custom is going to force you into marriage. Singlehood is an entirely respectable condition. Some people ask, "How can a relationship be open and fulfilling when it is maintained by legal fiat?" But it is no longer an obligation imposed from outside by society, it is one into which two people freely agree to enter. It is a commitment that has been freely chosen, not the loss of freedom to some external compulsion. To the question, "Are you staying together because you love each other or because you have to?" a married couple may reply, "We're staying together because we love each other enough to prefer a situation in which we are bound to stay together." They freely choose to take a step together that will place restraints on their freedom in the future, a rational step that will probably limit the immediate satisfaction of instinctual desires for one or both of them later on, a step taken when they can see the best of each other that will prevent them from abandoning each other when they are confronted with the worst, a step taken by each when strong that will ensure the comfort of the other in adversity.

Much of the tragedy of marriage—particularly when it is

undertaken with the romantic idea that a ceremony with pretty dresses and tuxedos ensures lasting happiness—is due to thinking of it as an ending, whereas it is a beginning. Or, to be accurate, it is a critical staging place. Marriage should be the point at which two people have become sufficiently sure of each other to risk the advantages and disadvantages of sharing their lives fully and permanently. Marriage is not a status but a journey, not a static model on top of a cake but a life-long exploration, not a set of photographs but an adventure. It involves readiness to participate in the growth of another person and opening oneself to the joy and the pain of being changed by and with the other. As Clayton Barbeau puts it, marriage is an art form, "The most challenging and complex of all the works a human being can be inspired to create." Or to use another analogy that I owe to a recently translated book by Pope John Paul II, it is a continual birth and rebirth: "Even when a new human being cannot be born from the union of a man and woman, or from a particular occasion of sexual intercourse, the spouses are none the less reborn in love, and so to speak give birth to each other in their interpersonal communion." A marriage relationship can meet the human need for trust, criticism, support and caring better than any other arrangement anyone has come up with. As a group of marriage counselors put it in a discussion: "The one-to-one commitment is hard as hell, but no viable alternative presents itself that is as rewarding, as intimate, and as significant."

But the question can properly be asked: "Why does this need to be public? Why isn't a private agreement to live together sufficient? Why introduce ceremonies and legal documents and rings?" The answer is that it is the formal, public, permanent nature of the wedding vow that often sustains a marriage relationship when almost any private, informal arrangement would be subject to intolerable strains. Any relationship involves periods of ennui, occasions of crisis, and situations that inhibit rather than encourage growth. Married people who are mature and realistic often discover that it is only because they have made a prior public commitment that they survive these threats (including sexual diversions), and through them discover new resources of healing. We find that we only know what love really means when we have confronted its most insidious dangers. Love grows through surviving tests which, in the immediate heat of deceit or misunderstanding or anger, appear to be insurmountable. Love, in the subjective darkness of conflict, needs the sustaining objectivity of a rationally willed decision. It is not enough, therefore, to make a commitment "so long as our love shall last" because the lasting of love depends upon the fact that the commitment was made "so long as we both shall live." It doesn't matter that in our time there is an escape route (through divorce) if love finally fails: what does matter is that love's survival and renewal is often made possible precisely because the use of that escape route is more difficult than the effort required to struggle through the winter of love's discontent.

However inadequately it may be expressed in many wedding ceremonies, a marriage is an occasion on which the couple not only help themselves by "going public," but an occasion on which they ask for the commitment of their friends and relatives, to support them in their vows. There may be times when both of them "want out" but witnesses to their original intention can recall for them how it was in the beginning. And in a wider sense, by giving public expression to their relationship a couple acknowledges that love and marriage are not private affairs. The problems of excessive dependence on each other and isolation from the community in cohabitation arise largely from the fact that that is not a publicly recognized arrangement. In marriage, as one author put it, the couple says in effect: "Not only are we emotionally tied to each other, but the evidence of our good faith is that we want the world to share in the knowledge of our life together and to hold us responsible within our common social existence for the vows we make to each other."

To quote one young wife: "To marry, to celebrate a love and a commitment publicly, in the presence of family and friends, is to say that the meaning of one's life can only be found in the context of a community. It is to acknowledge one's part in the human family, to recognize that one's life is more than one's own, that one's actions affect more than oneself. It is to proclaim that marriage is more than a private affair between one woman and one man." No mature people can be satisfied merely with the intensification of love within the dyad. A couple sealed within the space of their internal concerns will suffocate from lack of oxygen. *Philia* and *agape* can only feed nutrients to *eros* if their roots reach outside the hothouse of domestic togetherness. And one obvious way in which a couple can interact with and contribute to the human family is through the family they may create. Although parenthood is no longer the primary goal of many marriages and children are doubtless contraindicated for some couples, marriage remains the most satisfactory medium for the nurture and education of children, and parenthood can greatly enrich people's lives. On the other hand, a couple's growth in mutuality is likely to be tested to the full by children, and if society wants to strengthen the family it had better provide child-care for working mothers rather than attempt to return prayer to the schools or women to "total marriage." Love can survive parenthood and emerge the stronger for it, but those who think of having children as a way to salvage a shaky relationship need their heads examined.

I assumed in the past that living together would enable people to make better marriages and prepare them for the long-term demands of love. I didn't see how your generation could do much worse than mine, and cohabitation seemed to offer the prospect of a more realistic approach to marriage and a better basis on which to make the choice of a life-partner. Some experts share this view and believe that cohabitants are better equipped to deal with intimacy and more able to communicate with a partner. But others who have studied or counseled married couples who had previously cohabited conclude that it has little impact on marriage, except to delay it. It is certainly no panacea, and if you and Jim decide to live together remember it isn't a real test of your marital compatibility. You can't have a trial marriage any more than you can have a trial baby. You take on most of the problems of marriage without the support that marriage can provide. And you avoid some of the real tensions that marriage involves as a byproduct of its permanence. For example, it is not so easy to treat a partner's less attractive habits lightly when you are bound to him or her for life. One woman recently said, "We lived together so long, and I'd managed to put up with his gambling all that time. After we got married, though, what was acceptable and even a little exciting in a lover turned out not to be what I wanted in a husband." So don't start cohabitation without recognizing how much like marriage it will be, and don't ever get married without recognizing how unlike cohabitation it will be.

Further Reading

Altmann, Dennis, *Homosexual—Oppression and Liberation*, Avon, 1971.
Arieti, Silvano, *The Will to Be Human*, Quadrangle, 1972.
Barbach, Lonnie Garfield, *For Yourself—The Fulfillment of Female Sexuality*, Anchor, 1976.
Barbach, Lonnie and Levine, Linda, *Shared Intimacies*, Doubleday, 1980.
Barbeau, Clayton D., *Creative Marriage*, Seabury, 1976.
Bardwick, Judith M., *Psychology of Women*, Harper & Row, 1971.
Bengis, Ingrid, *Combat in the Erogenous Zone*, Knopf, 1972.
Bernard, Jessie, *The Sex Game*, Prentice-Hall, 1968.
Boston Women's Health Book Collective, *Our Bodies, Our Selves*, Simon and Schuster, 1973.
Boswell, John, *Christianity, Social Tolerance, and Homosexuality*, Chicago, 1980.
Brownmiller, Susan, *Against Our Will*, Simon and Schuster, 1975.
Buber, Martin, *I and Thou*, Scribner's, 1970.
Calderone, Mary S. and Johnson, Eric W., *The Family Book About Sexuality*, Harper & Row, 1981.
Caster, Lawrence, "This Thing Called Love Is Pathological," in *Psychology Today*, December 1969.
Daly, Mary, *Beyond God the Father*, Beacon, 1973.
Drabble, Margaret, *The Waterfall*, Knopf, 1969.
Feldman, David M., *Birth Control in Jewish Law*, New York University Press, 1968.
Fletcher, Joseph, *Situation Ethics*, Westminster, 1966.
Ford, Clellan S. and Beach, Frank A., *Patterns of Sexual Behavior*, Harper & Row, 1970.
Freud, Sigmund, *Three Contributions to the Theory of Sex*, Dutton, 1962.
———, *Introductory Lectures on Psychoanalysis*, Liveright, 1979.
Friedan, Betty, *The Second Stage*, Summit, 1981.
Fromm, Erich, *The Art of Loving*, Bantam, 1963.
Gould, Lois, *Such Good Friends*, Dell, 1978.
Grant, Vernon W., *Falling In Love*, Springer, 1976.
Greene, Gael, *Sex and the College Girl*, Dell, 1964.
Greer, Germaine, *The Female Eunuch*, McGraw-Hill, 1971.
———, "Seduction is a Four-Letter Word," in *Playboy*, January 1973.

Hamilton, William, *The Christian Man*, Westminster, 1956.

Heckinger, Grace and Heckinger, Fred M., "Homosexuality on Campus," in *The New York Times Magazine*, March 12, 1978.

Hite, Shere, *The Hite Report*, Macmillan, 1976.

———, *The Hite Report on Male Sexuality*, Knopf, 1981.

Hunt, Morton, *Sexual Behavior in the 1970s*, Playboy, 1974.

J, *The Sensuous Woman*, Dell, 1971.

John Paul II, Pope, *Love and Responsibility*, Farrar, Straus and Giroux, 1981.

Kelly, Janis, "Sister Love: An Exploration of the Need for Homosexual Experience," in *The Family Coordinator*, October 1972.

Kephart, William, "Evaluation of Romantic Love," in *Medical Aspects of Human Sexuality*, February 1973.

Kinsey, Alfred C., *et al.*, *Sexual Behavior in the Human Female*, Saunders, 1953.

———, *Sexual Behavior in the Human Male*, Saunders, 1948.

Kirkendall, Lester, *Premarital Intercourse and Interpersonal Relationships*, Julian, 1961.

Kosnik, Anthony et al., *Human Sexuality*, Paulist Press, 1977.

Lorenz, Konrad, *On Aggression*, Bantam, 1967.

Lower, George, *Feelings of Regret Involved in Premarital Intercourse*, privately printed.

Maccoby, Eleanor E. and Jacklin, Carol N., *The Psychology of Sex Differences*, Stanford, 1974.

Macklin, Eleanor, "Heterosexual Cohabitation among Unmarried College Students," in *The Family Coordinator*, October 1972.

Mailer, Norman, *The Prisoner of Sex*, Signet, 1971.

Malinowski, Bronislaw, *Sex and Repression in Savage Society*, Routledge & Kegan Paul, 1960.

Marmor, Judd, ed., *Homosexual Behavior*, Basic, 1980.

Maslow, Abraham, *Toward a Psychology of Being*, Van Nostrand, 1962.

Masters, William H. and Johnson, Virginia E., *Homosexuality in Perspective*, Little, Brown, 1979.

———, *Human Sexual Inadequacy*, Little Brown, 1970.

———, *Human Sexual Response*, Little, Brown, 1966.

May, Rollo, *Psychology and the Human Dilemma*, Van Nostrand, 1966.

———, *Love and Will*, Norton, 1969.

Mayeroff, Milton, *On Caring*, Harper & Row, 1971.

McNeill, John J., *The Church and the Homosexual*, Andrews and McMeel, 1976.

Mead, Margaret, *Sex and Temperament in Three Primitive Societies*, Mentor, 1950.

Midgley, Mary, *Beast and Man*, Cornell, 1978.

Morris, Desmond, *The Naked Ape*, McGraw-Hill, 1967.

Noonan, John T., Jr., *Contraception*, Harvard, 1965.

O'Neil, Robert P. and Donovan, Michael A., *Sexuality and Moral Responsibility*, Corpus, 1968.

Phipps, William E., *Was Jesus Married?* Harper & Row, 1970.

Saghir, Marcel T. and Robins, Eli, "Clinical Aspects of Female Homosexuality," in *Homosexual Behavior*, Judd Marmor, ed., Basic, 1980.

Sarrel, Lorna J. and Sarrel, Philip M., *Sexual Unfolding*, Little, Brown, 1979.

Schaefer, Leah Cahan, *Women and Sex*, Pantheon, 1973.

Seaman, Barbara, *Free and Female*, Coward, McCann and Geoghegan, 1972.

Sherfey, Mary Jane, *The Nature and Evolution of Female Sexuality*, Random House, 1972.

Steinem, Gloria, "The Moral Disarmament of Betty Coed," in *Esquire*, September 1972.

Storr, Anthony, *The Integrity of the Personality*, Penguin, 1963.

————, *Sexual Deviation*, Penguin, 1964.

Symons, Donald, *The Evolution of Human Sexuality*, Oxford, 1979.

Tax, Meredith, "The Woman and Her Mind: The Story of Everyday Life," in *Notes from the Second Year: Women's Liberation* ed. Koedt, 1970.

Tripp, C.A., *The Homosexual Matrix*, McGraw-Hill, 1975.

Unsworth, Richard, ed., *Sexuality and the Human Community*, United Presbyterian Church, 1970.

Wilson, Edward O., *On Human Nature*, Harvard, 1978.

Acknowledgments

I am greatly indebted to many people who read the manuscript of this book and made helpful corrections and comments: Robert Bennett, Lynn and Jim Borgman, Sol Gordon, Graham and Karen Hettlinger, Lester Kirkendall, Eleanore Luckey, David Mace, Patsy Ong, Elizabeth and Josephine Rice, Philip Sarrel, Carrie Stilwell and Carolyn Wilson. Mary Hettlinger, Elizabeth Emmert, Polly Wagner and Carolyn Wilson helped with resource materials. The staffs of the Kenyon College Bookshop and the Gordon Keith Chalmers Memorial Library provided valuable technical assistance. Lee Wilson typed the manuscript with her usual skill and remarkable speed. I am especially indebted to my wife, Mary Hettlinger, who is herself active in sex education and family planning, and who has contributed much to the ideas in this book.

I have made considerable use, for illustrative purposes, of *The Hite Report* on female sexuality and the companion volume, *The Hite Report on Male Sexuality*. They have been criticized for being unrepresentative of the general population and for being statistically imprecise. However, no study of sexual attitudes is truly random or altogether objective. Hite's findings seem to me particularly significant because they represent the thinking and behavior of the more educated and liberal segments of the population. The comments of her respondents certainly reflect attitudes common among college-level women and men and they bear, as one reviewer put it, "the stamp of passionate (even painful) honesty." Some of the personal statements I have quoted without other identification come from the two Hite volumes.

INDEX

134: